R

The

UPROOTING

of

EUROPEAN
IDENTITY

Edited by

RICHARD B. SPENCER

Radix Journal
Washington Summit Publishers
2012/16

Washington Summit Publishers
PO Box 100563
Arlington VA 22210

email : Hello@WashSummit.com
web : www.RadixJournal.com

Cataloging-in-Publication Data is on file
with the Library of Congress

ISBN: 978-1-59368-053-4
eISBN: 978-1-59368-011-4

Printed in the United States of America
10 9 8 7 6 5 4 3 2
2nd Printing

For Jonathan Bowden

[vi]

RICHARD B. SPENCER
is former Assistant Editor at
The American Conservative
and Executive Editor at *Taki's
Magazine* (Takimag.com). He
founded *Alternative Right* and
Radix Journal and is Director of
The National Policy Institute and
Washington Summit Publishers.

Statement
Richard B. Spencer

This volume marks

the debut of *Radix Journal*—a periodical on culture, history, politics, spirituality, and society. The name "Radix" has already been established as an imprint of Washington Summit Publishers. While WSP proper focuses on the scientific study of man, Radix publishes fiction, criticism, and writings on the intersection of genetics, culture, and society. *Radix Journal* will make space for an even greater variety of perspectives.

The journal will also distinguish itself through its structure. Though produced at regular intervals, each issue will be dedicated to a central theme or question—and in this way, stand on its own. We believe this is the proper role for the print journal in the 21st century. "The Death of Print" has become a tired cliché in a world of blogs, social networks, and mobile computing; and it is a notion we do not find satisfactory. Though pulp and ink have certainly given way to the Web and pixels as the primary means of communication, this hardly means that print is dead. Indeed, liberated from utilitarian concerns, books and journals can focus on beautiful typesetting, longevity of interest, and the experience of the reader. Each issue of *Radix Journal* will become, we hope, something to which the reader will return. Blogs are gone with the wind; *Radix Journal* won't be. (That said, digital copies will be made available.)

The choice of the name is also significant. "Radix" is, of course, Latin, meaning "root" or "stem." It is the basis of a number of familiar "roots" words, including "radish" and "race." "Radix" also gives us "radical," a word which is often abused. The "extremist"—that is, he who takes things too far—is one thing; the "radical," in the true sense of the word, is another. He is not excessive, but instead uncovers the heart of the matter; he searches out the source. In a Nietzschean sense, the radical is a physician who looks beyond mere symptoms and uncovers the disease. We hope each issue of *Radix Journal* will live up to the name.

Radix I's theme is the uprooting of European, White identity worldwide—in terms of culture, politics, and historical heritage. It ultimately entails the destruction of Europeans as a unique biological entity.

Though it was not planned this way at the outset, South Africa—and the Boer people, in particular—serves as a *Leitmotif* throughout the collection. It seems that in the ghettos and security fences of contemporary Johannesburg, and in plucky Boer ethno-communities like Orania, one sees the worldwide status of the White man laid bare. He faces formidable challenges; the greatest of which is not, in fact, demographic decline, but that he has become the *Zeitgeist*'s favorite villain—indeed, the White man has become a villain to himself.

Beyond the crisis in South Africa, the experience of European peoples worldwide can be said to be distinctly "post-Apartheid," "post-colonial," and "post-national." The White man lives in a world his race once dominated—and in which Black and Brown are now colonizers, in which European heritage is being taken away piece by piece: cultural heroes, literature, popular icons, identity—ultimately, everything. The Boers themselves can be counted as exceptional in this regard, for, as Andy Nowicki and Derek Turner explore, they are actively resisting these trends and have not lost their self-respect and will to survive.

We hope that *Radix Journal*, too, will mark an act of resistance (however meager). And subsequent issues will move beyond the gloomy, though essential, task of diagnosing what's wrong. For the mission of the radical is not just to understand the world . . . but to change it.

UPDATE—OCTOBER 2016

The original title of this book, when it was published in early 2012, was *The Great Erasure*. For the second printing in 2016, which includes many corrections but no substantial changes, the title was changed to *The Uprooting of European Identity*. The rationale is simple. "The Great Erasure" is a brilliant and evocative meme, and in 2017 it will be used as the title for a introductory volume, which will cover the concept of "White Genocide" and the cultural disposseion of European people throughout the world.

The

GREAT
ERASURE

ALEX KURTAGIC

*"Immigration" is no
longer an adequate term
to describe the social,
political, and racial
transformation resulting
from mass migration.*

ALEX KURTAGIC
is a publisher, cultural
commentator, novelist, musician,
and artist. He is the author of the
dystopian novel, *Mister* (2010),
the founder and director of
Supernal Music, and Editor-in-
Chief of Wermod & Wermod
Publishing Group.

[4]

Much of the debate

on the decline of Whites in their traditional homelands centers on "immigration," and specifically the continuing arrival in the West of large numbers of colored "immigrants" from the poorest regions of the world. But is "immigration" an accurate term for this phenomenon?

Some critics of "immigration" feel the term is euphemistic and prefer to label the phenomenon "invasion." Guillaume Faye calls it "colonization." Yet, although the use of alternative terminology is motivated by legitimate concerns with the scale, the permanence, and the non-assimilation associated with modern immigration in the West, neither alternative seems satisfactory.

First, the scale of immigration does not alter the nature of the phenomenon, as the definition of "immigration" still holds so long as it describes individuals moving from one polity to another for purposes of establishing residence. Secondly, length of residence does not transform immigration into something else, as immigration does not exclude, and, indeed, often involves, permanent relocation. Thirdly, assimilation is separate from, and not a condition for, successful immigration, even if it is so for integration. Furthermore, both invaders and colonizers can be immigrants, but immigrants are not necessarily invaders or colonizers (and they are neither if they appeal to the established sovereignty for admission, inclusion, and integration.)

[6]   Indeed, "invasion" is wide of the mark. In a geopolitical sense, an invasion is an aggressive military operation aimed at "conquering, liberating, or re-establishing control or authority over a territory, forcing the partition of a country, altering the established government or gaining concessions from said government, or a combination thereof."[1] In a biological sense, the term still involves aggression. Modern "immigration" in the West, though it may have similar effects, and though some "immigrants" may be aggressive, is neither military in character nor centrally organized—save exceptionally and loosely—by either active or passive encouragement to emigrate and resettle in a specific polity or territory.

---

[1]   "Invasion," Wikipedia.org, accessed September 1, 2012, http://en.wikipedia.org/wiki/Invasion.

"Colonization" is much closer to the mark, but still not on it. The term refers to the establishment of colonies in one territory by people from another territory, but colonies can comprise colonists or colonials, the latter of which is linked to colonialism. In colonialism, a metropole claims sovereignty over the colony, deliberately changing—when the territory is already inhabited—the social structure, government, and economics of the colonized territory. "Immigration" is not "colonization" in this sense. Arguably, "immigrants" into the West have increasingly sought to gain or exert control over the social structure, government, and economics of their host countries, but they are not—save with one exception, mentioned below— subjects of a metropole with a deliberate policy of colonization. The "immigrants" issue from multiple metropoles, which are uncoordinated, geographically dispersed, may be rivals or enemies, and in all but one case operate no policy of colonization, officially or unofficially. Moreover, the so-called "immigrants" are not even coordinated among themselves, beyond temporary subjection by some or exploitation by criminal gangs of human traffickers. The "immigrants" are impelled, not by a single-minded desire to establish or join a colony, but by a variety of individual motives, mostly involving escape from danger or poverty in their native territory and a desire for safety and (above all) economic betterment in a prosperous metropole.

The term "colonization," however, is not entirely inadequate, for modern "immigration" in the West still involves exogenous strangers colonizing Western polities. This is because, while different from colonialism, structurally the phenomenon remains related to it. A more apt term for the phenomenon of "immigration" would be "settler colonialism," which can involve settlers from multiple metropoles whose behavior and consciousness is very similar to that of our modern Third World "immigrants"; but the term remains problematic, since it describes projects like Israel today, South Africa up until the early 20th century, and what eventually became the United States, from the 17th century through most of the 19th. Nevertheless, "settler colonialism" is structurally most similar to what is discussed in this essay, however, and provides a sound theoretical basis for what I propose to call, for the purposes of distinction, "settler colonization."

[8]

In this essay, I will first provide a description of settler colonialism as it is currently theorized. I will then show how settler colonialism closely describes modern "immigration" in the West. Next, I will indicate how the Western experience with modern settlers from the Third World differs from that of past settler-colonial projects. Finally, I will suggest possible strategies for combating settler colonization in our hemisphere.

SETTLER COLONIALISM

Edward Cavanagh, editor of the *Settler Colonial Studies* journal, and Lorenzo Veracini, author of *Settler Colonialism: A Theoretical Overview*,[2] define settler colonialism as follows:

---

[2]   Basingstoke: Palgrave, 2010.

Settler colonialism is a global and transnational phenomenon, and as much a thing of the past as a thing of the present. There is no such thing as neo-settler colonialism or post-settler colonialism because settler colonialism is a resilient formation that rarely ends. Not all migrants are settlers; as Patrick Wolfe has noted, settlers come to stay. They are founders of political orders who carry with them a distinct sovereign capacity. And settler colonialism is not colonialism: settlers want Indigenous people to vanish (but can make use of their labour before they are made to disappear). Sometimes settler colonial forms operate within colonial ones, sometimes they subvert them, sometimes they replace them. But even if colonialism and settler colonialism interpenetrate and overlap, they remain separate as they co-define each other. [9]

In his book, Veracini also ascribes to settler colonialism distinctive characteristics:

- Settler colonialism creates a dual division between itself, exogenous Others, and indigenous Others; these can be either virtuous or degraded.

- Settler colonialism is always virtuous, always forward-moving, conceiving itself and its activity in terms of improvement and progress. Indigenous Others are rarely virtuous, but can be either elevated or degraded, while exogenous Others can be selectively included or segregated. However, settler colonialism more easily includes exogenous Others than indigenous Others and routinely fantasizes about exchanging indigenous Others with exogenous Others.

- Inclusion and exclusion operate concomitantly, attraction and revulsion operate concurrently, without a need for consistency. Yet, while borders are internally porous, they are externally impermeable: settlers can go out, but indigenes cannot get in.

- Settler colonialism involves the settler self undergoing coeval processes of indigenization and exogenization.

- Settler colonialism thus converges with the original society, but the line is never crossed because the distinction needs to remain.

- Settler colonialism dominates in order to transfer (remove); colonialism dominates in order to exploit.

- Settler colonialism tends to underestimate the indigenous in various objective and subjective ways, making the indigenous invisible.

- Settler colonialism, accordingly, subjectively conceives areas to be annexed or opened for settlement as vacant.

- Settler colonialism sees itself as ultimately, if not immediately, autonomous, and therefore resists interference from the metropole; colonialism is subordinate to the metropole.

- Settler colonialism is characterized by an exclusive interpretation of peoplehood, a specific understanding of sovereign capacities and their location, even though settlement itself is messy and most people move individually, "without a conscious determination to establish a new, ideal, society, and with no specific understanding of their own sovereignty."[3]

- Settler colonialism sees the settler colonial setting as charged with a special regenerative nature.

- Settler colonialism is characterized by the ability to will a collective identity and its institutions into existence.

- Settlers come to work and live in peace and see themselves as escaping from violence; a secure future in the new land is recurrently and dialectically opposed to an uncertain prospect in the old one.

- Settler colonialism disavows its violent foundation, but peacefulness coexists with violence.

- Settler colonialism suffers from "ongoing concerns with existential threats and a paranoid fear of ultimate decolonization."[4]

- Settler colonialism has a linear structure, whereas colonialism has a circular structure: for one, the

[11]

---

[3] *Ibid.*, 54.

[4] *Ibid.*, 81.

literary metaphor is the *Aeneid*, for the other, the *Odyssey*; one involves non-discovery, since settlers simply reproduce their society; the other, discovery, since the discoverer reports back to the metropole; one involves *non-encounter* with the indigenous (they are invisible, shadows, undercounted, deterritorialized, sojourners, part of the landscape), the other *encounter* (through exploitation).

- Settler colonialism, because it deterritorializes the indigenous and denies their state-forming capacity, can be superseded only by itself, ending with the complete elimination of the indigenous. In this case, the end is negotiated from within, including complicated and dubious processes of "national reconciliation." The alternative ending is settler exodus or expulsion. In this case, there is never equality or any subsequent relationship between the indigenous and the settlers; settler colonialism is a winner-takes-all scenario: either the indigenous or the settlers disappear. Colonialism, on the other hand, ends with state formation (by the indigenous), and its end is a negotiation between states (the colonizers' and the indigenous').

- Settler independence accelerates the process of nation-building and hence the process of erasure of the indigenous. Even well-meaning acts of reconciliation and incorporation entail the erasure of indigenous forms as it occurs in the context of settlers' forms.

[12]

SETTLER COLONIZATION IN THE WEST

As has been noted, critics of "immigration" in the West have noted its unprecedented scale, its permanent character, and the non-assimilation/non-assimilability of Third World "immigrants." Among the characteristics of settler colonialism is that settlers come to stay and do not appeal to the established indigenous sovereignty, but rather deny it and seek to remove it in order to replace it with a reproduction or regeneration of their own society. Implied in settler colonialism is scale: settlers may arrive as individual immigrants, but the process of reproduction, removal, and replacement necessitates sufficient scale successfully to neutralise, overcome, and eliminate indigenous resistance.

[13]

In Western Europe this is most apparent in the continuing growth of Islamic formations by immigrant Muslims, who, now numbering in the millions, found and daily operate their own structures in parallel with the indigenous authority. Spread across the regions, but concentrated in metropolitan enclaves, these structures may be physical, such as mosques and madrassas, or they may be legal-theological, such as arbitration tribunals based on Shariah law. Their prosperity benefits from demographic contraction and loss of faith by Europeans, whose churches are gradually converted into mosques; but it is also driven by a will to conquer the land, which, from time to time, find open expression across a range of settings, from the streets to high political office held by Muslims. During the disturbances caused by the publication of a cartoon of the prophet Mohammed in Denmark in 2005, Muslim protesters variously called for Shariah law for the United Kingdom, worldwide domination by Islam, the death or slaughter of those who insult Islam, and the extermination of Europeans. Similarly, in 2008, Labour politician Shahid Malik, former Justice Minister and Minister for Race, Faith and Community Cohesion at the Department for Communities and Local Government, stated at that year's "Global Peace and Unity" conference, held at the Excel London Centre:

> *I am proud of the achievements of Muslims in this country from '97. In 1997 we got our first Muslim MP. In 2001 we had two Muslim MPs. In 2005 we had four Muslim MPs.* In ša Allah, *in 2009-10, we'll have eight Muslim MPs. In 2014 we'll have sixteen Muslim MPs. At this rate, the whole Parliament will be Muslim! But just to say, in case there are journalists here today, that is not my objective. But you know, we've got four Muslim MPs; there should be* twenty *Muslim MPs in Parliament. And* in ša Allah *very shortly we'll see that. I am confident, as Britain's first Muslim Minister, that, in ša Allah, in the next thirty years or so, we'll see a Prime Minister in this country, who happens to share my faith.*

[14]

Such messages cannot be dismissed as simple expressions of anger or hopeful prognostication. Anger and hope can be expressed in many ways, and it is significant that, rather than calling for respect and toleration of a Muslim minority, the thrust of the messages, be it from protestors or from a Justice Minister, flowed uniformly in the direction of conquest, replacement, and Islamic supremacy.

In the United States, Mexican immigrants of recent decades have a well-documented history of forming their own parallel structures. In their case, it takes the form of businesses, pressure groups, student organizations, printed and electronic media, gangs, and social networks permeating occupations, neighborhoods, and local politics, within which all transactions and interactions are conducted in Spanish. Mexican immigrants, their descendants (including naturalized ones), as well as Mexicans in Mexico, also conceive themselves, even at official government level, as possessing a sovereign capacity as Mexicans—"I have said that Mexico does not stop at its border, that wherever there is a Mexican, there is Mexico." A true Mexican immigrant leaves Mexico behind and appeals to the United States government so that he may eventually become an American; a Mexican *settler* takes Mexico with him, and, though he may take up American citizenship, the latter is done for purely instrumental (*e.g.*, economic) reasons. Some more ideologically racialist Mexicans dream of replacing the United States government with a Chicano superstate to be called "Aztlan." A more common assumption of Mexican settlers is that part or all of the U.S. will gradually transform into a more lucrative version of their home country.

[15]

The process of replacement is made partially invisible by its interaction with a vestigial European settler colonial consciousness: "immigrants" have slowly built their structures largely in the shadows, persistently undercounted and underestimated. This is an instance where settler colonialism and settler colonization interpenetrate.

Third World settlers in the West replicate the dual division of peoples in settler colonial projects, and the relationship between self and other is analogous. Upon arrival, they are faced with indigenous Others, who comprise the majority and are ostensibly the established authority, as well as with exogenous Others, who comprise minorities of fellow travelers and against whom they are now pitted in competition for resources and admission by the established authority. When faced with real or perceived resistance by the indigenous, settlers perceive themselves in a shared predicament with exogenous Others. This makes them more receptive to establishing friendships or alliances with exogenous Others against the indigenous established authority. Said exogenous Others, however, may be found within structures of the established authority itself. Thus, generic pro-"immigrant" pressure groups emerge with the backing of establishment politicians. (As discussed further below, these politicians, though exogenous, may also be or appear to be indigenous.)

The consciousness of settler colonization in the West is always virtuous: settlers seek employment, economic betterment, educational improvement, professional progress, and a peaceful life. Indigenous Others are rarely virtuous: they are racists, bigots, Islamophobes, infidels, faithless, and degenerate. They can, however, be elevated by converting to the settler's faith and/or cause. They can, by adopting their manners and sensibilities, also be selectively admitted into the settler collective, including through marriage, although this may require conversion. In the latter case, reluctant admission and desire for admission interpenetrate, for the settler, still perceiving himself as less powerful than the indigenous (even if more virtuous), sees acceptance as a gateway for deeper colonization and altering the indigenous society in ways more amenable to his collective (*e.g.* by campaigning for "anti-racist" legislation). When settlers run for political office, one part of them desires acceptance by the establishment (it is powerful and confers privilege), another desires to change that establishment (it is racist and excludes settlers). It is not gaining admission with a view to assimilating to the indigenous Other, but rather gaining admission with a view to neutralise and/or displace him.

Thus, inclusion by and of the settler and exclusion of the indigenous operate concomitantly, attraction and revulsion operating concurrently and without consistency. [17]

The search for admission, even if without a view to assimilation, does involve a process of indigenization. The indigenous in Europe, because they tend towards individualism and low ethnocentricity, confuse indigenization of the settler with assimilation, not realizing that settlers are ethnocentric collectivists and seek eventually to recast European society in their image. The process of indigenization involves settlers becoming the indigenous, not settlers becoming *like* the indigenous (even though the former does superficially involve and necessitate the latter to varying degrees.)

A process of exogenization of the settler in relation to the latter's original society is the other facet of his indigenization in Europe, for as he indigenizes in an alien environment, he also diverges from the members of his race, whom he has left behind. The evolution of past settler colonial projects, particularly those involving multiple races and ethnicities, such as what became the United States, point to the eventual emergence of a sense of peoplehood, albeit qualified by racial or ethnic membership. This means that while the United Kingdom may variously converge with India, Pakistan, Africa, and the Caribbean, settlers from these countries or regions, and more so their descendants, and particularly where they are racially mixed, will not see themselves as subjects or indigenous to those countries and regions, but as British citizens indigenous to Britain, whose heritage goes back to one or more of those countries or regions. It follows from this that while there will be convergence, the line will never be crossed because the distinction will always remain.

[18]

While the end result is the transference (removal) of the indigenous, settler colonization in the West coexists with exploitative relationships proper of straight colonialism. It is well known that Third World settlers in the West, even at the appellant stage, take advantage of the indigenous' welfare state and concessionary provisions, and that these benefits are often a reason for immigrating in the first place; indeed, on the whole, these settlers consume more than they produce. However, exploitation is not limited to scrounging from the indigenous government: it also takes the form of various forms of ethnically organized fraud, such as car crash insurance claim scams, which are run by Muslim gangs, or ethnically organized exploitation, such as pedophilia, also associated with Muslim gangs. So long as the indigenous remain in charge, they remain both an obstacle and a resource.

This is linked both to the subjective underestimation of the indigenous and the conception of Europe as vacant. Although the latter may seem an exaggeration, it is not if we understand ethnocentricity as involving a certain "vacating" (or evacuation) of the Other's humanity. Third World settlers in the West are by nature highly ethnocentric, at least in relation to the indigenous White majority. The West is thus conceived by settlers primarily as a space, a land, where there are resources and opportunity, not as comprising people just like them who can provide generosity and friendship. The indigenous Westerner, therefore, is vacant, present but absent, a somewhat abstract entity that has to be dealt with, if only because "it" holds the "keys to the kingdom," but which is otherwise denied and subjectively disappears until the next time "it" gets in the way or the settler realizes he needs something from "it." The indigenous White majority is essentially part of the landscape, but, as with irredentist Mexican settlers in the United States, it can be seen as sojourners, interlopers, or usurpers.

[19]

Both the emergent sense of peoplehood, even if multifarious and complicated by racial and ethnic divides and miscegenation, and the conception of a vacant land of opportunity, are concurrent with autonomy from the originating metropole, and even resistance to its interference. It must be borne in mind that many settlers immigrate as economic or political refugees, and seek to make a new life in the Western *El Dorado*. Making a new life is another way of saying regeneration; the West, and immigration to the West, are imbued with a regenerative nature. In turn, this regeneration occurs as a dual process, whereby the settler regenerates (that is, generates again) his own society and simultaneously has his life regenerated in (and/or by) the land of opportunity. Given the often dysfunctional nature of Third World societies, this duality would seem to be mutually negating, since the society being regenerated is the society from which the settler fled, and a successful regeneration of that society would impede the successful regeneration of the settler's life. Indeed, a secure future in the new land is recurrently and dialectically opposed to an uncertain prospect in the old one. But settlers do not require consistency.

[20]

Third World settlers immigrating into the West are motivated primarily by the prospect of economic betterment; they have no specific understanding of their sovereignty and neither do they, with the exception of politicized Mexican settlers in the United States, possess a conscious collective will, for settlers move individually, even if they arrive in groups. All the same, as we have seen from the proliferation of parallel substitutive formations by settlers in the West, they do possess the ability to will a collective identity and its institutions into existence.

The process of doing so is non-violent, following a legal sequence comprising: appeal to the indigenous authority (for recognition and admission as permanent minorities, and eventually citizens); development of exogenous structures (serving as substitutes to indigenous ones); co-option of indigenous structures (lobbying for concessions, multiculturalism); subversion from without (lobbying for anti-racist legislation); and indigenization (becoming legislators, subversion from within). At the same time, the process coexists with violence, whereby the indigenous are physically attacked or subject to predations (typically muggings, robberies, racially motivated beatings, and rape), or else morally attacked (typically accusations of prejudice and "racism," and/or "racism" hoaxes).

Conversely, settlers live in paranoid fear. In the West, colored settlers imagine themselves in the midst of indigenous "racists," in an institutionally "racist" society, even though said society has invited them, granted them recognition, made concessions, opened its labour market to them, accepted them as citizens, elected them into public offices, denounced "racism" in all its forms, swiftly purged "racists" upon detection, and even changed its laws to criminalise "racism" and punish "racists" with added rigor. This may be because settlers both have a well-developed sense of racial identity, because they would never welcome colonization in their traditional homeland, and because they are routinely agitated by ideologically egalitarian fanatics. No matter what gains they make, the fear of "racism" is ever present, and the perceived risk of expulsion (decolonization) ever lingering. In both Europe and the United States, it has happened before: in 1492 (the Spanish *Reconquista*) and 1954 (Operation Wetback).

[21]

Expulsion or a mass exodus would, indeed, be the only way to end Third World settler colonization in the West. Millions of settlers are citizens, many going back several generations, not a few descended from mixed race marriages. Short of expulsion or a mass exodus, the long-term effect of settler colonization, aided by high numbers of incomers and differential fertility favouring the settlers, is the replacement of the indigenous population. The latter will not need to disappear entirely, at least as a biological entity, before being completely dispossessed: even without violence, the indigenous institutions of democracy and equality provide the logic and mechanisms for dispossession. If the majority of people in Britain are Muslim, for example, democracy necessitates that they be proportionally represented in the seats of political, economic, cultural, academic, and institutional power. The historical rarity and fugaciousness of democracy in the Third World, however, suggests that democratic governance would end as soon as it ceases to be useful for the settlers, though this is not to say that the indigenous could not well dispense with it in the face of an immediate existential threat—democracy has proven historically rare and fugacious in the West, too.

[22]

Without the complete erasure of the indigenous Westerners, the end of Third World settler colonization in the West would at best imply a dubious procedure of "national reconciliation," involving negotiation by the indigenous with triumphant settlers from within, and in the context of settlers' established forms. Most likely, given the multiracial character of settler colonization in the West, is that one ethnicity would gain the ascendancy over all the others, and it would be they who become the new indigenous. The Bantus in South Africa provide a historical example.

UNIQUENESS OF SETTLER COLONIZATION IN THE WEST

Settler colonization in the West is not unique because of its scale or the fact that settlers are poor. Settler colonialist projects have involved large numbers in the past and many of the settlers have been poor—in most cases, they immigrated looking for a better life. The uniqueness of our experience with settler colonization results from the unique features of modern Western societies.

[23]

First, it is the colonization of the more powerful by the less powerful, of the former colonialists by the formerly colonized; it is, in other words, a reversion of past colonialism and settler colonialism.

Secondly, this process enjoys the ongoing complicity of the indigenous' ruling elites, who, wittingly or unwittingly, instigated it in the first place out of a perceived economic need, and have since institutionalized it out of political opportunism, greed, a sense of historical guilt, or befuddlement with an ideology of human universalism. The opening of land to colonists by leaders is not unique: African kings in southern

Africa either sold or gave away land to European settlers in exchange for military service during the 19th century. What is unique is the institutionalization of a policy of welcoming settler colonization, supported by a universalist ideology that makes the voluntary transfer of land and sovereignty morally virtuous.

Thirdly, alongside indigenous collaborationism, Third World settler colonization in the West has been catalyzed by both historical events and the existence of a hostile or at least self-serving exogenous minority of very able intellectuals, businessmen, and legislators. The excesses of the National Socialist government in Germany during the 1930s and 1940s, Allied victory in World War II, and the moral capital amassed and exploited by Jews—and especially radical Marxist Jews— as a result of well publicized National Socialist persecution, permitted the development of Jewish intellectual movements that subjected traditional European identity and institutions to radical critiques. Their effect was the gradual deprecation of European tradition and racial identity and the development of universalism to its logical extreme. Interacting with guilt as the primary method of social control in the West, this made it possible even for genetically distant immigrants eventually to become legislators because it had become impossible for the indigenous to argue against exclusion based on race.[5]

[24]

---

[5]   See Kevin MacDonald, *The Culture of Critique: An Evolutionary Analysis of Jewish Involvement in Twentieth-Century Intellectual and Political Movements* (Westport, Conn.: Praeger, 1998); Paul Gottfried, *Multiculturalism and the Politics of Guilt: Towards a Secular Theocracy* (Columbia, Mo.: University of Missouri Press 2002).

Fourthly, the sovereignty transfers take a more abstract form than the land leases, cessions, seizure, or annexations that have characterized settler colonialist projects elsewhere. In the West transfers occur at the legal, policy, and moral-philosophical levels; they involve, for example, changes in legislation that privilege settlers over the indigenous, abdication of indigenous racial consciousness as a morally legitimate cognitive structure, or discrimination policies against the indigenous designed disproportionately to enhance settlers' access to higher education and the job market. Similarly, the emptiness and evacuation of the "land of opportunity" among settlers occurs at a much more abstract level than allowed by indigenous demographic contraction: the Western "land of opportunity" is densely populated and highly developed, so the evacuation is purely subjective. Its closest analogue is modern Israel, where the "promised land" is subjectively emptied by denying Palestinians the same moral and symbolic status as Jews.

[25]

Finally, the settler colonization in the West does not involve the ignoring or direct overrunning of the indigenous, but rather an incremental engagement, which runs concomitantly with a process of gradual transformation of the settler from appellant to citizen to legislator, which is, in turn, wrapped up with the process of indigenization already mentioned.

Third World settler colonization of the West is possible only as a result of a uniquely Western ideology (egalitarianism) and an autochthonous political system (democracy), both of which morally and ideologically disarm the indigenous against settler ascendancy and predation.

ENDING SETTLER COLONIZATION

As has been noted, settler colonialism rarely ends, and it is superseded only by itself. After the United States' independence, the former settlers ceased to be colonials from a distant mother country because their mother country had become the United States. Moreover, the indigenous were in time either displaced or made to disappear entirely, so there was no question of the indigenous regaining their independence and the colonials returning home—as just stated, the latter were at home. Third World settler colonization in the West being analogous, it follows that the crisis faced by Westerners is much more fundamental than simple out-of-control immigration. A polity can exclude immigrants and strip resident immigrants of their citizenship, but settlers are founders of polities, so they cannot be stripped of their own citizenship by the displaced indigenes, since the indigenous sovereignty is not recognized.

It should be apparent that we in the West live still in a time of transition, where immigration coexists with and interpenetrates settler colonization, and where one has not entirely given way to the other. Yet it is already possible for a citizen of South Asian or Afro-Caribbean descent in the United Kingdom to treat, for example, a White South African over the age of 16 immigrating into the island as a foreigner, and to be in a position to grant or deny admittance, even where the South African has blood ties to the island going back thousands of years and was born to United Kingdom citizens. Conversely, it is no longer possible, without an abrogation of modern Westernism's basic philosophical tenets, suddenly to withdraw citizenship from a United Kingdom resident descended from one or more generations of South Asian or Afro-Caribbean citizens. Even the overnight expulsion of illegal immigrants and the passing of the most restrictive immigration law imaginable in our present ideological context could not deal with this problem. As time passes, the immigration reform debate will become increasingly irrelevant.

Where settler colonialism was terminated or reversed, such as in South Africa after Nelson Mandela, Rhodesia after Robert Mugabe, and Haïti after Jean-Jacques Dessalines, the measures required were violent and broke (or would have broken had it existed) current international law. Because this law is premised on equality as an absolute moral good, reversing settler colonization in the West would, without first abrogating this law, or else discrediting the moral basis for such body of law, also imply violent and illegal acts. Settler colonization is, after all, a game of erasure: settlers erase or are erased; no ongoing or equitable relationship is possible between settlers and indigenes. And the single biggest impediment to Whites' avoiding erasure is the hegemonic belief in the West in *equality* as an absolute moral good, because the latter dictates that settlers be accorded equal rights and privileges to the indigenous (despite settlers being

[27]

hostile), and because this belief effectively short-circuits the possibility of an opposing belief in the morality of White racial consciousness and preservation.

Whites in Europe and North America, as well as in former colonies in Africa, the South Pacific, and South America, currently lack a moral theory, let alone the legal means (since the latter would stem from the former), with which to justify and secure their continuity. Unless a new moral theory of *difference* can be formulated to support an ideology and legal framework that both justifies and enables its self-preservation as a unique biological entity in their own homelands, the White race faces complete erasure from the Earth. ৺

The

NIGGERS

of the

EARTH

ANDY NOWICKI

Andy Nowicki
travels to South
Africa to report on
the life of the Boer
people and White
survival in the
Rainbow Nation.

ANDY NOWICKI

is the author of the novels
*Considering Suicide, The Columbine
Pilgrim,* and *The Doctor and the
Heretic.* He is a regular contributor
to *The Last Ditch* and *Alternative
Right,* and has published work for
New Oxford Review and *American
Renaissance.* He teaches college-
level English and lives in Savannah,
Georgia, with his wife and two
children. He also intermittently
contributes to his blog when the
spirit moves him to do so.

[*images*]
"Geloftedag"
Orania, South Africa
Andy Nowicki (2011)

"Nelson Mandela Dr."
Johannesburg, South Africa
Andy Nowicki (2011)

"Voortrekker Monument"
Pretoria, South Africa
Andy Nowicki (2011)

If you're out of luck or out of work
We can send you to Johannesburg.

Though I am neither out of luck nor work at the [33]

time, these lyrics from the Elvis Costello song "Oliver's Army" nevertheless keep turning through my head during my grueling 15-hour flight from Atlanta, Georgia, to the notorious South African metropolis in question. When Costello recorded this pop-punk classic, a deceptively sweet-sounding jazzed-up calypso tune harshly critiquing British military imperialism, the name of Jo'burg was synonymous with the White Afrikaner Apartheid regime, then still clinging to power. Back in the 1980s, it seemed that everyone and his mother knew all about the odious ideology practiced by the ruling National Party of South Africa. Apartheid was held, in the court of world public opinion, to somehow be a *uniquely* awful practice, as bad, in its own way, as Nazism had been. It was viewed with such loathing that South

Africa in effect became the nigger of the world: ostracized from trade, banned from the Olympics, shunned by right-thinking people everywhere. Forget the Soviet Union, China, North Korea, and other repressive, murderous Communist regimes (so we were instructed by liberal opinion-shapers), it was *South Africa* alone which truly deserved our greatest contempt. Apartheid, after all, was racial repression, dominance of Blacks by Whites, and therefore fascist, and therefore *neo-Nazi*, and therefore another Holocaust in the making, which must be stopped at all costs.

Cue movies like *Lethal Weapon II*, *A Dry, White Season*, and *Cry Freedom*, egregiously simplistic cinematic morality plays with noble and magic Negro/White liberal heroes and hateful, mean-faced, invariably *Afrikaner* villains. Cue also Artists United Against Apartheid's silly protest anthem "I ain't gonna play Sun City," ("Relocation to a phony homeland/ Separation of families, I can't understand" being among its resplendent lyrics.) And cue the faithful, unthinking, conformist allegiance of the sheeple towards the "respectable" party line.

To be fair, Apartheid was a lousy ideology, deeply flawed in conception, and often brutal in practice. But any saving sense of proportion, whereby one acknowledged that, compared to the rest of Africa, under various bizarre and ghoulish post-colonial regimes run by Idi Amin and other crackpot native-born dictators, Blacks actually prospered in Apartheid-era South Africa, and that repression in that country, while deplorable, was relatively mild compared with the tyranny of most Eastern bloc nations of the period.

The Afrikaners—descendants of the original White (Dutch, German, and French) settlers of the African continent and original creators of Apartheid as an official state policy following the victory of D.F. Malan over Jan Smuts in the 1948 election—have long absorbed my interest, for reasons that must relate in some way to the outcast status imposed upon them by self-righteous rock stars and international leftist activist-celebrities of the Reagan-Thatcher era. I have a soft spot in my heart for such unreconstructed "niggers of the world"-types, who thumb their noses at the "consensus" of the imposed *Zeitgeist*, and are hated and pilloried ever after for their effrontery, which is invariably construed as some sort of hateful and repugnant term with a suffix of *-ism* or *-ia* (racism, sexism, nativism, homophobia, etc). In the degenerate White West today, no one is ostracized more than an alleged thought-criminal, who rejects the *a priori* tenets of political correctness, and who remains unmoved by *ad hominem* assaults upon his integrity stemming from his refusal to toe the party line.

[35]

Though I don't consider myself a cultural American Southerner, I always enjoy seeing Southerners proudly fly the "stars and bars" of the Confederate Battle Flag, in brazen, stubborn defiance of the edicts of their societal "betters." As an English teacher and writer, I have actively opposed the culturally-Marxist linguistic scourge of "inclusive language," which demands that we say "humankind" instead of "mankind," or "fire-fighter" instead of "fireman," as well as determinedly rejecting the designs of "diversity" czars who want to dethrone the "Dead White Male" Western canon and have us all reading crappy books written by semi-literate Aboriginal Eskimo albino lesbian hunchbacked cripples out of deference to a specious "inclusivity."

For almost half a century, the Afrikaner presented a "nigger"-face to a Western world, growing more and more inured to militant modernist liberalism. The Afrikaner wasn't simply a "racist," who rejected multiculturalism for favor of thoroughgoing racial separatism; he was also a strongly *religious* sort of chap, as well. Now modern-day liberals can tolerate conspicuous manifestations of religious fervor, provided that they're expressed by people who aren't White, but anytime ethnically-conscious Whiteness and specifically *Christian* religiosity are combined, the militantly tolerant multiculturalist tends to get all in a snit. After all, weren't Hitler and the Nazis Christians, as well? (They actually weren't, but then you can't expect a modern-day liberal, busy as he is with conscientiously correcting the prejudice and ignorance of his less enlightened neighbors, to be bothered with questioning his own numerous unfounded prejudices or addressing his often grievous historical ignorance.)

[36]

The Afrikaners, being the "niggers of the world," had won my sympathy nearly two decades ago, after their leaders caved to world pressure and dethroned themselves, Lear-like, handing the kingdom over to their enemies. Now, in December 2011, I am finally getting to meet my far-flung soulmates. On the generous dime of my benefactors at the National Policy Institute, I am jetting across the world, leaving the relatively safe confines of the good-ol' U.S. of A. for the southern tip of the Dark Continent, to experience these "niggers" firsthand, now adrift in their formerly recognizable homeland, wandering like poor, homeless, mad King Lear through a gathering, apocalyptic storm.

§

These days, following the implosion of the Apartheid regime and the advent of true "democracy" in 1994, which has ushered in nearly two decades of rule by the Black-dominated African National Congress, Johannesburg is newly notorious... as the rape and murder capital of the world. For this reason, I—a nervous flyer—feel a strange combination of relief and apprehension as we touch down at O.R. Tambo (formerly Jan Smuts) airport. "Out of the frying pan, into the fire," is a phrase that thrusts itself into my exhausted mind as I file out of the plane and shuffle through customs alongside my weary fellow travelers.

[37]

Of course, I am being overly dramatic. Johannesburg is a very dangerous city, but (much lurid tabloid-like propaganda to the contrary) it isn't exactly a war zone. If you exercise proper caution and avoid doing foolish or reckless things or going to obviously dodgy locations, you should be fine. Still, one is immediately struck by the extent to which living and working units in the area are conspicuously *fortified*. Nearly every private residence and business location in the Gauteng province—an area which includes Jo'burg and its sister city Pretoria, as well as the infamous Black township Soweto—is a mini castle-keep, complete with a high palisades electric fence, with barbed wires curlicued across the top, and one security company or another advertised prominently at the front. No resident of the area can simply visit a neighbor by walking up to his front door and knocking or ringing the doorbell; instead, you have to buzz in at the front entrance, and wait for your neighbor to trust that you aren't a thief, a murderer, or a rapist, before allowing you to obtain entrance by activating the automatic gate.

One is tempted to wonder if this setup isn't a hysterical overreaction on the part of Whites to the undeniably real crime problem in South Africa. But the more I talked to individual Afrikaners, the more I felt inclined to believe that these fastidious security precautions are eminently reasonable, even necessary. It seemed that everyone had a horror story of some form or fashion to tell, either of a family member or a friend, on a farm or in a city or in a sleepy suburban locale, who became a victim of an awful act of aggravated violence. . . A cousin of one man sat in his home watching a rugby match on TV on a Sunday afternoon, when suddenly a gang of Black thugs entered—one of them made a run at his wife in the living room, and as he rushed to protect her, he was shot and killed... A woman's uncle and aunt were savagely tortured and murdered in their home one night—nothing was even stolen from the house. . . A fellow in his mid-30s relates that a young friend of his once stopped to assist a group of young Black men on the roadway whose car had supposedly broken down; in so doing, he walked right into an ambush—the men attempted an armed robbery, and the friend of the woman was gunned down in the ensuing melee. . . Another man opens up about how his girlfriend was carjacked in broad daylight—she found herself set upon by four Blacks with guns at a busy intersection; fearing a gang rape, she left the keys in the ignition and fled in a panic. A mother tells me of a girl who was suddenly set upon by a Black man with a machete, who hacked her to death without provocation on a dark street one night.

Then there are the less shocking, more numerous accounts of petty muggings here and there, ever-present "smash and grab" raids, whereby a criminal walks up to an unsuspecting motorist, shatters his window with a crowbar or other solid object, reaches in to snatch the driver's purse or Blackberry from the dashboard or passenger seat, or simple home burglaries which take place while the homeowner is at work or out of town.

[39]

$

To be sure, Afrikaners and other Whites aren't the only victims of crime—many decent, law-abiding Blacks have also been robbed, raped, and murdered—but there seems evidence to deduce that native Blacks have turned on the Boer nation—their former rulers—with particularly hateful ferocity. Indeed, illegal and nominally legal activity seem to stem from a similar motivation. The democratically-elected ANC government changes the names of Afrikaans roads and cities in a transparent effort to punish the people who they felt oppressed them in the past, and imposes ruthless and insane racial quotas upon businesses and social services—even to the point where, for example, prospective black doctors in medical school are held to far less rigorous standards than their White counterparts, in order to increase the representation of Black doctors (never mind, I suppose, how well they treat the sick!). White farmers (predominantly Afrikaner) are asked to cede ever more of their private property in the interests of agricultural affirmative action; meanwhile, farm murders continue apace in a steady, dreary campaign of terror. Children are raped; elderly couples are made to drink acid and set on fire; one hears of new, blood-curdling attacks nearly every month. According to credible statistics, there have been nearly 2,000 murders of farmers and their family members since 1991, and the numbers, while fluctuating from year to year, show no signs of abating.

Many have become convinced that the government is in fact behind the murders, whether through deliberate manipulation or as a result of irresponsible, vindictive anti-White rhetoric and propaganda, creating an atmosphere of hate. In Pretoria, I spoke with three representatives of the Transvaal Agricultural Union (TAU), who openly declare their strong suspicion that some governmental authorities are complicit in the killings. General director Bennie van Zyl noted that many of the murders seem to take place in areas where the ANC has agitated for a greater degree of "land reform." (Under the stipulations of "Black Economic Empowerment," or "BEE" policies, farmers are required to let their black employees have part of their land after a certain number of years of employment.)

"There is certainly a link between violent attacks on farms and land claims," declares van Zyl. "In provinces where the land claims are big, the attacks are big."

Van Zyl draws a link between what is happening to Afrikaner farmers in South Africa and what has happened all over the continent from time to time when one tribe or group seeks to dispossess another, the most egregious recent example being the savage massacre of the Tutsis by the Hutus in Rwanda in the mid-'90s.

[41]

"It's a pattern in the whole of Africa," he says. "And I don't think that the Western world recognizes this pattern. It's very hard for us Afrikaners to understand it, and we grew up with those guys (the Blacks)."

Using language that would make most North American and European Westerners, liberal or otherwise, blanch and titter as if they'd just heard a dirty joke, Van Zyl claims that in his view, it is simply a part of the African's nature and mindset to conduct such murderous campaigns.

"We (White Afrikaners) believe in God, but they (Blacks) believe in the power of their ancestors," Van Zyl says. "We accept responsibility, while they replace responsibility. Their leaders want them to be perceived as a people with a deep-seated value system that attaches value to life, but the practice is very different."

The world largely knows about the depredations of Robert Mugabe and his Zanu-PF Party in neighboring Zimbabwe. In that country, Mugabe's forces have systematically forced the White farmers off of their land, bankrupting many and physically attacking others. As a result, a once relatively prosperous African country has turned into a blighted, impoverished scourge of a land. When I ask if South Africa might become the next Zimbabwe, the representatives of the TAU respond that it's already happening, simply in a covert manner.

[42]   "It's a case of a velvet glove covering an iron hand," says TAU service manager Chris van Zyl.

I shed my liberal leftism long ago, in my undergraduate years, and today I call myself a moderate racialist, yet I find myself discomfited by the implication that Black Africans have some sort of natural proclivity towards ruthless violence. I also find it hard to accept that the ANC, incompetent and corrupt as it may be, has actually organized a murderous campaign against White farmers. I admit as much to these men, who in response own that not all Blacks are culturally depraved; many, in fact, are perfectly nice people. However, they also ruefully note that the current ruling political party of South Africa—one of whose rally songs is "Kill the Boer, Kill the Farmer"—isn't exactly falling over itself trying to make a priority of stopping the farm murders, or stopping Black-on-White violent crime in general. Even if they aren't directly complicit, they claim, the African National Congress has very little interest, if any, in protecting Afrikaners from harm.

"If there is crime, it suits the ANC," says Bennie van Zyl. "The purpose of terrorism is to terrorize."

§

During the time I spend in Johannesburg and neighboring Pretoria, the word "surreal" keeps leaping to mind. It's just hard to get a handle on this strange place. There is dire talk of continuing Black-on-White crime and even whispers of a coming Rwanda-style attempted genocide, an event supposedly predicted by legendary Afrikaner seer and mystic Nicholaas "Siener" van Rensburg, a kind of Boer Nostradamus who allegedly predicted the assassinations of Koos De La Rey and Hendrik Verwoerd, the advent of Black rule in South Africa and the bitter blossoming of the deadly and virulent AIDS epidemic. Though the Afrikaner nation is largely religious, spiritual devotion does not equate to superstitious credulity; not all buy into the "van Rensburg-as-prophet" notion. Yet there are mounting fears of a widespread, racially-motivated *Kristallnacht*-like "purge" against Whites taking place in the near future, whether provoked by official anti-Afrikaner ANC rhetoric, or merely as the result of uncontrolled mob violence following some galvanizing event (such as the death of Nelson Mandela) or mounting Black frustration over

[43]

unemployment and poverty (which haven't improved and have in fact largely worsened since Mandela's election in 1994, but both of which are still commonly blamed on the "legacy of Apartheid" and White racism and colonialism).

Such fears of a looming mass slaughter strike me as lurid and overblown, even paranoid. Then again, this is Africa, where terrifying tribal violence has been, and continues to be, commonplace. It's difficult to picture the world not intervening while Black mobs massacre Afrikaners in the streets all across South Africa...then again, "the world" largely *didn't* intervene when Hutus slaughtered millions of Tutsis in Rwanda back in the mid-'90s. Nor has the "world" openly condemned the unrestrained violence against the South African farmer since the ascendancy of the ANC. But expectations of such impending horrors would be easier to digest if much of the country didn't still strike this visitor as fairly "normal," orderly, and familiar, in a modern, Western sense. You can, after all, find in this country all of the amenities most First Worlders have come to expect as their birthright. South Africa has posh shopping malls, hip coffee houses, state-of-the-art movie theaters (with stadium seating), fast food restaurants, and well-stocked gas stations (though they call them "garages"). It has cable television, Internet service, and operational traffic lights (called "robots").

[44]

Yet if you allow yourself to get lulled into complacency by all of this seemingly civilized Western-style prosperity, you might be in for a nasty shock. For example, if you spend too much time lost in thought at a red-lighted "robot," you might suddenly find yourself carjacked, kidnapped, or sexually assaulted. This is a country where one is advised to run a red light in certain locations if possible, since to stop, that is to say, to *obey* the given traffic laws, means to make oneself vulnerable to property theft or bodily harm. It is a country in which many drivers plaster their vehicles with "Baby On Board" bumper stickers, not, as in America, in order to shame other motorists into driving safely around them, but rather to beg potential criminals to allow them to take their child out of his harness in the event of a carjacking!

§

I only have to imbibe this schizophrenia-inducing atmosphere—whereby, day after day, one hopes for tranquil normalcy while at the same time gravely fearing a sudden spasm of violent calamity—for a mere two weeks, and it nearly wears me out. One night I wake from ambiguously horrifying nightmares, gasping desperately for air, having been briefly assailed with some variation of cerebral shell-shock. If merely visiting South Africa produces such a reaction in a person, then how much more severe must be the psychic response to actually *living* here?

[45]

Dan Roodt, a distinguished writer and long-standing Afrikaner activist, meets me at an upscale "garage" halfway between Jo'burg and Pretoria. As we sit together and munch on our sandwiches, he reflects on what he calls this "extremely bizarre" set of contemporary circumstances in his country.

"In South Africa, we have the most violent peacetime society in the world," Roodt says. "It's almost like a low-intensity war. And there is always a risk that some incident could trigger riots and unrest."

Roodt blames the "climate of hate" created by an ANC-dominated education system, which he holds responsible for much of the virulent racial antagonism raging among the country's citizens today.

"South African Blacks are more anti-White than any population in the world," he observes. "It's a part of this whole 'victim' mentality. The ANC has created a fictional past 'reality' that feeds the present violence."

[46]

By endlessly harping on the supposed evils of past White rule, and at the same time cynically playing on base tribal superstitions (President Zuma recently told voters that their ancestors would afflict them with sickness if they voted against the ANC in coming elections), the present rulers of South Africa have "ensured that they'll never be voted out of office," Roodt owns. At the same time, he says, many Blacks old enough to remember the Apartheid years will admit that, in many ways, things were better for them then than they are now.

"They (the Blacks) had jobs back then, and things were predictable," Roodt says. "Social services were competent, unlike now," he adds, noting the collapse of infrastructure and the graft, corruption, and incompetency that runs rampant among members of the current government.

Roodt is a lean, elegantly handsome, rather patrician-looking 54-year old man with a full head of thick silver hair and a gentle, unassuming, soft-spoken manner that seems, in some ways, at odds with his passionate, at times almost strident rhetoric. Like many Afrikaner intellectuals his age and older, Roodt began his academic career as a man of the Left, furiously critical of the National Party and its Apartheid policies, only later to take a severe right-ward turn following the ascension of the ANC to power and the troubled times that followed.

"Our generation had the sense that our parents were conformists," he says, recalling his turbulent adolescent years. "There was a sense of rebellion at the time. At our schools, some of the older teachers were bullies who abused their authority over us... Once I began rebelling against the way things were, I just went further and further."

[47]

In fact, Roodt went all the way to Paris, France, in part to avoid being conscripted into the armed forces and forced to take part in the border wars South Africa was fighting against hostile Communist-backed neighboring regimes at the time. But he eventually became dismayed by the brazen ignorance and despicable malice displayed by many of his Parisian comrades-in-arms.

"That was my first reality check," he reflects. "These people I came to know looked at South Africa in a completely simplistic way." Their perspective, in fact, was ludicrously "black-and-white": that is to say, the Whites were brutal oppressors, and the Blacks were noble and righteous seekers of justice and liberation.

Roodt became irritated by such instances of typically leftist hive-minded groupthink, and he also began to resent how his home country got assailed with one economic sanction after another by country after country as the years rolled by. "Why should we be singled out for ignominy, when other countries have *much* worse human rights records?" he asked others at the time, never obtaining a satisfactory answer.

Then came the crucial turning point of his self-imposed exile from South Africa. In the late 1980s, Roodt was invited to meet with the cultural section of the African National Congress in a seminar set up by a certain left-wing "liberation theology"-minded church group in Germany. His experiences at this seminar led him to suspect that an ANC takeover would be disastrous to those of his ethnic and racial background.

[48]

"Even though I was still a trendy, liberal literary scholar, I felt a sense of rejection from the Blacks and Coloureds present," he recalls. "That sent me thinking. On the way back from Germany, I realized that I couldn't betray my own people to become one of these unreconstructed Communists."

These days, Roodt is contemplating the best way to continue the struggle for Afrikaner self-determination. Among other projects, including forays into politics, he has alighted upon a (literally) novel concept: he is in the early stages of composing a science fiction manuscript, set on another planet in a distant future, that explains the contemporary clash of races in an allegorical sense. Through such an unusual format, Roodt said he hopes to open minds that are currently paralyzed by rigidly enforced PC dogma surrounding the issue of racial differences.

"I'm at the stage where I feel like I need to do something extraordinary to change people's minds," he says.

§

Foremost among the goals of Roodt and others like him is to forge an authentic Afrikaner homeland, a place where the descendents of the historic "Boers" can feel safe and can be assured of their legitimate interests being protected. Nearly everyone I spoke with in Jo'burg and Pretoria said that they found the current state of things utterly untenable. Most feared [49] creeping demographic disaster through massive emigration and low birthrates, continued economic disenfranchisement through relentlessly applied government-sponsored affirmative action and so-called land "reform," and rising violence against their persons and property in the form of Black crime and terrorism.

Yet for all of the problems the 21st Century Afrikaner faces from without, his stubborn, individualistic streak hampers him from bonding with his kin and facing his enemies in a united front. An oft-heard, somewhat bitter joke I heard on several occasions from many sources, each independent of the others, runs thusly:

Q: *What do you get when you put three Afrikaners on a desert island?*

A: *You get four different churches, and five different political parties.*

Though there is much difference of opinion regarding which path to take out of the current quandary, there seems to be a general consensus that accepting the status quo indefinitely is a recipe for both individual and collective disaster, if not for eventual ethnic extinction. Desperation hangs so thickly in the air that one can almost smell it. To many, it seems the future holds only the bleakest of prospects. Several hundreds of thousands of Afrikaners have emigrated from their home country to other places in the world since 1994—and even earlier, when the proverbial writing was on the wall that the Apartheid-era government was in its death throes.

Yet while many have left the country (and the continent) for such distant destinations as New Zealand, Australia, England, Canada, and America, and others have retreated within their heavily fortified homes behind barbedwire fences and electric gates, hoping for the best while steeling themselves for the worst, a relatively small number of contemporary Afrikaners have opted to pursue a radical, risky, but potentially more rewarding course of action. Some, that is, have staked their hopes on the prospect of seceding from the current wreck of a "Rainbow Nation," and constructing a kind of Boer ethno-state in its very midst, with the intention of reclaiming their genetic and cultural self-determination, and saving the Afrikaner identity from dilution and eventual extinction.

Currently, two such communities exist, though there is talk of more attempts to be launched in the near future.

Kleinfontein is essentially a Pretoria suburb, located near "Diamond Hill," the site of a legendary battle in the Anglo-Boer War. Orania, which has garnered much more national and international attention, can be found along an unassuming country road in the arid "karoo" of the Northern Cape. Both towns are 100 percent Afrikaner in ethnic composition, and the traditional Afrikaans language—an intriguingly uber-guttural tongue sometimes described as "bastard Dutch"—is proudly spoken and fiercely promoted.

The short-term game plan of both Kleinfontein and Orania, of course, is to peacefully coexist with the South African governmental powers-that-be, not to brashly declare themselves inheritors of a new nation, as if spoiling for a fight. One gathers, however, that the leaders of both communities are keeping a sharp eye on social and political trends and measuring their prospects for political independence in the near future, should present cultural deterioration continue apace. Needless to say, the greater the peril that Afrikaners feel themselves to be facing in their day-to-day lives, the more attractive such radical living options will start to appear, and the more Afrikaners flock to places like Kleinfontein and Orania, the harder it will be for such communities to avoid being seen as dangerously insubordinate hotbeds of rebellion against good "Rainbow Nation" values. For now, however, both towns are basically left alone.

[51]

Kleinfontein is a fascinating and impressively-conceived, if dusty and somewhat hardscrabble little place, full of winding dirt roads and rambling country houses, protected by a pair of guards and a checkpoint at the entrance. A statue of Hendrik Verwoerd—former South African prime minister and fervent Apartheid organizer and promoter—stands at the center of the town square. Verwoerd, who was brutally stabbed to death by a crazed Coloured man in the House of Assembly in Cape Town back in 1966, is an object of veneration to residents of both Kleinfontein and Orania, though both communities heavily reject the man's policy of mandating racial segregation by law, if for no other reason than that it wound up making the Afrikaner spoiled and "soft," reliant on other ethnicities to cook his food, clean his house, tend his garden, and otherwise perform his menial tasks. The insistence that the Boer people need to relearn self-reliance was a constant refrain, one I heard emphasized by nearly everyone. One particularly mordant joke manages to reference both the fear of Black crime and apprehension that the modern-day Boer has lost the hardy, self-sufficient will that so characterized his intrepid Voortrekker ancestors. . .

Q: *Who is an Afrikaner today?*

A: *Someone who'd rather get murdered in his bed than make it himself.*

Kleinfontein's founders hold that Gauteng is the most opportune province in which to establish a new Boer homeland, as the greater Pretoria region remains the place most heavily populated by self-identified Afrikaners. Still, even in Gauteng, the percentage of Afrikaners is quite low with respect to the general population. Country-wide, recent estimates are that Whites make up only 9 percent of the current population of South Africa—that is to say, around 5 million people in a country of over 50 million citizens (with the untold numbers of non-White illegal immigrants pouring in daily through the porous northern border, rendering the Whites of the country even more racially outnumbered). Of that five million, it's estimated that around three-and a half million are of Afrikaner descent—the rest being chiefly British. With such dwindling minority status, Afrikaners zealous to maintain their heritage must take particular precautions.

With this in mind, the founders of Orania planned   [53]
ingeniously. They purchased land in the Northern Cape adjacent to the Orange River in the late 1980s, in sparsely populated country. Hendrik Verwoerd took pains during his lifetime much to insure that this dry land in this area be irrigated; upon Orania's establishment in 1991, its residents immediately began raising various crops and readying them for "export" to the rest of the nation, as well as to the world.

Today, Orania has grown impressively prosperous through sales of pecan nuts, alfalfa, wheat, maize, olives, apricots, and peaches, as well as through the manufacture of a diverse array of homemade products from jewelry to bricks to coffins. The population of Orania began quite small, but has grown incrementally through the years—now there are over a thousand residents, and many others who plan to move there in the future once they obtain the means and can obtain local work.

Kleinfontein and Orania are around the same size, but perceptions of late seem to be that Klienfontein has stagnated somewhat, while Orania looks to be poised for ever-greater growth and development. It is difficult to tell if such perceptions are based on anything solid, or are merely indications that Orania's founders and backers have run a cannier—and more ambitious—PR-campaign. In any case, I determine that my investigation of the current state of the Afrikaner nation would be incomplete without paying a visit to these mysterious and strangely alluring Oranians. I call ahead, book a room at a humble, rustic inn, rent a car, and one morning undertook my own "Great Trek" of sorts to a largely undiscovered country, seldom seen by American eyes.

§

The 350 mile drive from suburban Johannesburg to Orania proves to be exhausting. Partly this is due to the typical psychic discombobulation that inevitably ensues when a born-and-bred American driver suddenly has to get used to driving a car with the steering wheel on the right hand side of the car instead of the left, and of having to stick to the left-hand side of the road, rather than the right. But other factors don't help, either. For one thing, even in the suburbs one is constantly set upon by vendors hawking their wares—newspapers, pamphlets, maize stalks, and all sorts of worthless knickknacks—at every stoplight. Occasionally beggars get into the act; there is indeed a strikingly formal manner to African-style begging—they cup their hands together, as if in prayer, and bow their heads humbly to you, looking as pitiful as a sinner before an angry deity. You learn early on to wave them away with a firm gesture of determined disinterest, scrupulously avoiding eye contact all the while.

Then there are the roads themselves. Major South African roads look like American freeways around the cities, but once you get further out, they begin to more closely resemble lesser-used and less-well kept American state highways, complete with potholes and sudden detours into desultory little towns full of cracked plaster and strewn rubbish. The signage is often confusing, as well; I once followed an arrow on a sign which seemed to point towards the continuation of the road I wanted, but it actually steered me directly into a filthy, poverty-ravaged township. (When the road turned into dirt, I decided I must have misunderstood the where that arrow indicated that I go; I promptly whipped a "U-ie" (as they call such a maneuver around here) and found, after returning to the spot of the mistake, that the place I needed to turn was just after the road I'd mistakenly taken.

[55]

Hopping onto the N-12 outside of Jo'burg, I then pass through Potchefstroom, then proceed south through Warrenton and Kimberley, in whose dingy city center I temporarily lose the trail again. I have to turn several more U-ies before I regain sight of the N-12; I've again been thrown off by ambiguous signage in the midst of a dizzying series of twilit intersections. I pause to purchase a "Zinger Burger" from a roadside KFC (the most popular American fast food chain in this country), and once more head south towards Hopetown.

Hitting this lonely stretch in the gathering dusk, I soon find myself utterly in the dark for a good couple of hours. Here in the "karoo," the semi-desert terrain of the Northern Cape, towns are scarce, and this once major highway has essentially become a ragged country road. I grip the wheel, put my brights on when possible, and remind myself to "stay to the left, stay to the left, stay to the left." Occasionally trucks pass from the other direction with a zoom and a whoosh, and I briefly hyperventilate at the friction of what seems to be a near-sideswipe. Finally, at Hopetown I turned left on N-396 and in forty kilometers, at 10 p.m. I arrive in Orania, where it appears the entire town has gone to bed. John Strydom, the kindly if insistently industrious public relations officer of the town, escorts me through the rows of charmingly austere little houses and up a small hill, to where my accommodations have been prepared in a row of rooms still largely under construction.

[56]

The wind whips madly through the lonely brush as I grab my suitcase and stagger into my spare but clean little suite, overtired and a bit grumpy and frazzled from the arduous *trek* I'd just completed. Unlike the original Voortrekkers, I haven't had to ride in a creaky ox wagon or fight off Zulu *impis*, but I still feel worn out and down for the count.

I sleep well into the morning, but a buzzsaw from a nearby construction site provides a jarring wakeup call.

§

For the next three days, I explore Orania, talk with its residents and representatives, and take in the sights and sounds. I arrived with no preconceived notions, but I find myself surprised just the same. It seems, in many ways, a very ordinary country town: clean, safe, possibly even a little bit dull.

Indeed, those looking for evidence of a weirdly sinister right-wing neo-Nazi cult in Orania are likely to emerge disappointed. I found the place fairly well bursting with friendliness and pleasant vibes. One is struck, in fact, by just how *normal* these people seem. They aren't *freakishly* normal, in a 1950s *Leave It to Beaver* kind of way; they don't look like they've emerged from any sort of a time warp or temporal anomaly out of a *Twilight Zone* episode; they don't dress in ostentatious Victorian garb like characters in M. Night Shyamalan's *The Village*, nor are they clad in unflattering prairie dresses and long patriarchal beards like dwellers of some unsavory polygamous settlement in the heart of rural Utah. Instead, the Oranians wear contemporary clothes, sport modern hairstyles, listen to rock music and watch Hollywood movies. At the same time, they also seem focused on remaining *apart* from the larger society—indeed, it may be said that they practice a kind of voluntary "Apartheid," dedicated to "separate development" of a sort. Moreover, nearly all Oranians

[57]

seem to be quite religiously observant, though not all belong to the same church. Many are Dutch Reformed, the historical Calvinistic faith of the Afrikaner nation; others are members of the *Nederduisch Hervormede* Church or the *Gereformeerde* Church, the more traditional-minded and austere versions of the DRC; still others are members of various conservative "house churches." But whichever church body they call home, the Oranians agree to disagree on certain matters of theological doctrine and pull together around issues they view as crucial to their contemporary survival. And they feel that they can only ensure their survival and the continuance of their beloved traditions if they unite around a common vision of the *polity*, one that lays emphasis on both culture and ethnicity.

[58]

There is much gloom and doom among Afrikaners today regarding their prospects for the future, but the architects of the Orania project seem to grasp instinctively that a message of grim, militant pessimism doesn't sell well. The Orania campaign, thus, is to accentuate the positive. Posters around the town sing of Orania as a "dream come true." The most prominent promotional photograph depicts five pretty, long-legged teenage girls, each clad in orange, leaping joyously into the air, alongside the perky proclamation "Welcome To Orania!" The picture communicates youthfulness, vitality, innocence, even a kind of subtle (if wholesome) sex appeal. It causes the viewer to consider the town, not as a bitter refuge-spot for dead-enders, but as a *fun* place, where one can live free from care and dwell happily with one's brethren, and maybe meet a potential wife or husband.

And the pitch seems to be working: many do come to Orania, if only to stay temporarily. In addition to its export business of crops and commodities, around 30 percent of Orania's draw comes from the *tourist* industry. There is a fancy spa and a chalet-style motel, and an upscale restaurant overlooking the Orange River, along with a camping site. Guests commonly spend a night or two in the middle of a trip to or from Cape Town to relax and recharge. Thus, news of the existence and mission of Orania continues to spread via word of mouth.

The overwhelming majority of the people I meet in Orania prove to be welcoming and warmly accommodating. The fact that I'm an outsider ("uitlander"), that I don't speak the language, and that I'm there in the capacity of a *journalist* would all seem to be strikes against me. Orania has been overrun with newspaper and magazine writers over the course of its 20-year existence, and needless to say, most reporters have been of the "smirking liberal" variety—the type who are friendly and sympathetic to your face, take advantage of your sincerely offered hospitality, then proceed to write cruelly nasty articles about you. Despite the fact that the Oranians have no real reason to trust me, most are open with their thoughts, and only a rare specimen here or there seems in any way suspicious of my motives.

[59]

§

Perhaps the most interesting person I speak with during my stay in Orania is a shy, retiring, rigorously intellectual 36-year old man named Sebastiaan Biehl. One would normally expect a man of his cerebral bent to be found in academia; in Orania, however, he works as a real estate agent. Biehl is an *"uitlander"* who, one might say, has gone native. He is from Germany, but he has found his calling, to dwell among the Afrikaners—one might even say he is an Afrikaner convert of sorts. When I ask to confirm that he is German, he answers, "Yes, I was, originally." But he now considers himself a thoroughly naturalized Afrikaner; he speaks Afrikaans as a first language, and has even published a novel, entitled *Beslissing In Die Karoo*, in Afrikaans.

Biehl's journey began two decades ago, when he began to correspond with a pen pal who lived on a farm in the Free State province. When he visited in the summer of 1992, he said, it had the effect of a "revelation." Indeed, after working on his friend's farm for a couple of months, he had the sensation of finally having found his place in the world.

"I felt like I had come home," he recalls.

As a solitary, thoughtful lad, Biehl had long felt alienated from contemporary European mores. The erosion of faith in an increasingly secularized society had led, in his observation, to a culture that had grown "cold and immoral," rife with social ills.

Among the Afrikaners, Biehl says, he discovered "a deep-seated conservatism of the hearty sort," and at the same time he experienced "a rebirth or a rejuvenation of faith."

When he returned to the country of his birth, he came to perceive ever more clearly that he didn't belong there.

"I saw Germany with new eyes," he recalls. "I found it superficial and materialistic and hectic and... godless. I couldn't wait to get back to South Africa again. There was a feeling of freedom there, of wide open spaces. It was like stepping back in time."

He went to college at South Africa's Free State University in 1996, earning a degree in Political Science with a focus on History and Politics. Along the way, he changed his first name, adding an additional "a" to his given name of "Sebastian," in the Afrikaner style. After college, Biehl settled in Bloemfontein, [61] and then in 2005, after much soul searching, he opted to take up residence in Orania. He took a job as a realtor, though it had little relevance to his collegiate training, because he wished to choose a profession in which he could help his adopted hometown to grow and expand.

Biehl says he has absolutely no regrets about his radical lifestyle makeover. Though certain traits still mark him as an *"uitlander"*—he is, for example, a Lutheran in a community of Calvinists—he couldn't be happier than to dwell exactly where he does.

"Orania will always be where my roots are," he says. "You have to pay a price if you want to be free."

§

I have business in Gauteng before I return to the States, so I leave Orania behind on an early Sunday morning while everyone's at church, winding my way back to suburban Jo'burg. I opt, however, to spend an evening in the city of Bloemfontein to see the Women's Monument, a site first christened in 1913, dedicated to the remembrance of the women and children who were rounded up by the British during the Anglo-Boer War and dispatched to concentration camps, where many thousands starved to death.

[62]

The main fixture of the site is heart-grabbingly powerful. Before a massive obelisk, on a platform ten feet above the ground, there are three sculpted figures: a young woman bears a dead child in her arms, a desperately forlorn look upon her face; she is flanked by a middle-aged woman, who gazes into the distance stoically. As I stand at the foot of this statue, I find myself tearing up a bit; the simultaneous torment and determined endurance on the faces of the two stone women somehow says everything one needs to know about the horrors of "total" war and its dreadful victimization of the innocent.

During the Anglo-Boer war, the British resorted to horrifying atrocities in order to achieve domination over the scrappy Afrikaners; they slaughtered livestock, burned down farms, and doomed helpless civilians to sure, agonizing deaths. They weren't the first ones to do such things—Generals Sherman and Sheridan, under the command of Abraham Lincoln, decimated the American South in much the same manner half a century before. Nor was the British army the last to go "scorched earth" on its enemies, as all familiar with the bitter history of 20th-century warfare, and the hardly less horrifying first decade of the 21st century, can attest. But one cannot escape the sense that the British establishment of concentration camps represents some massively significant betrayal of ostensibly humane and "civilized" Western values, regardless of which side, the Brits or the Boers, had the more legitimate claim to political control over the Orange State and the Transvaal back in 1899. The Afrikaners suffered horrendously in this war, in manifold ways: physically, psychologically, and spiritually. Anger and bitterness for the wounds they endured at the hands of the British, in fact, still fester viciously to this day, over a century later.

[63]

§

Three days after viewing the Women's Monument in Bloemfontein, I visit another important Afrikaner landmark, and I once again find myself emotionally shaken, moved beyond measure for reasons I barely understand.

The Voortrekker Monument sits atop a hill in the outskirts of Pretoria. It is an imposing, cathedral-like edifice—somewhere near 130 feet tall—which can be viewed from a vast distance. In some ways, the Voortrekker Monument is the architectural antithesis of the Women's Monument. Completed and christened in 1949, it celebrates a major victory for ascendant Afrikanerdom just as the Women's Monument commemorates the horror and humiliation of an ignominious defeat. The year before, in 1948, the Afrikaner-favored National Party, led by D.F. Malan, defeated Jan Smuts, long-standing incumbent prime minister of the British-led United Party. A half century after losing the Anglo-Boer War, the Afrikaner had at last seized the upper hand and taken control.

Afrikaners tend to view Malan's electoral triumph of 1948 the same way that most of today's Black population sees Mandela's ascension to the South African presidency in 1994: it was a moment, following a great, decades-long struggle, in which they finally won what they felt to be their birthright. Crucial in building this victory was a canny campaign to celebrate the heroic valor of the Boer Voortrekkers of the previous century, who under the leadership of Andries Pretorius, won what they felt to be a miraculous victory over far-superior Zulu forces at Blood River in present day Kwazulu-Natal on December 16, 1838.

Prior to the battle, the Voortrekkers had suffered several terrible defeats on the veldt at the hands of Dingaan Zulu's mighty army, including a notorious "sucker-punch" ambush in which Dingaan invited Piet Retief and various other Voortrekkers to his camp under the auspices of signing a peace treaty, before directing his troops to torture and massacre the unarmed White men. Following this grievous incident, Zulu warriors conducted numerous destructive attacks on Voortrekker *laagers*, killing around 500 men, women and children.

Reeling with grief, and facing the prospect of impending utter extinction, the bedraggled camp of devoutly Christian pioneers led by Pretorius turned to prayer. On December 9, they took a vow, declaring before heaven that if God granted them victory in the coming battle, they would forever commemorate the date.

A week later, on December 16, the ragtag 480 Afrikaners turned away a fiercely invading force of Zulu *impis* numbering somewhere between 10,000 and 15,000, killing over 3,000 of their enemy and suffering not a single casualty in the process. It was afterwards hailed as *Geloftedag*, or "Day of the Vow."

Geloftedag is still a holy day in the traditional Afrikaner calendar, a day to remember the bravery and dedication of one's ancestors, as well as being a time to give thanks to the Almighty for his manifold blessings. It is like Thanksgiving, Veteran's Day, Passover, and the Fourth of July all rolled into one: a time for unabashedly celebrating one's national and ethnic heritage, while also engaging in solemn, sober spiritual reflection.

[65]

Geloftedag services are held in churches, parks, and other locations across the country, but the Voortrekker Monument is the largest and most publicized of all such venues. The building itself is an extraordinary enough place to investigate even on a quiet day. One ascends its massive staircase and walks along the length of its impressive exterior, scrutinizes its high stone walls flanked by massive statues of bearded Boers holding huge rifles, and one is filled with a sense of awe, as well as a kind of terror. This is a structure designed to *intimidate*; there is an undeniably *brutal* quality to its beauty. If the Voortrekker Monument had a voice, it would be low, loud, and thunderously threatening. This is the sort of building that Leni Reifenstahl would have loved to use as a set piece. To call it an example of "Fascist architecture" may be misleading, since ideological affinities between National Party-led South Africa and Nazi Germany are quite tenuous, for reasons already mentioned. Still, just as the National Socialists in Germany chanted *"Seig Hiel"* at their rallies, the Voortrekker Monument unashamedly demands that we "hail" a glorious "victory" for the Afrikaner tribe in South Africa.

If one objects that everything seems crudely simplistic and shamelessly triumphalist in tone, it could reasonably be retorted that all sites dedicated to national accomplishments and ideals—from Mount Rushmore to Trafalgar Square to the Arc de Triomphe—share this characteristically unselfconscious "hurray for our side" spirit of chauvinistic bravado. Today, of course, in our politically correct "post-colonial" age, historically White nations are discouraged from indulging in such sentiments, thus lending the Voortrekker Monument a rather delicious air of ripe, forbidden fruit.

The majestic interior contains a marble frieze which runs across the wall from one side to the other—a pictorial history is presented of the Voortrekker movement. We see the Boers leave the Cape and escape British tyranny to forge a destiny for themselves in the wilds of a savage and untamed continent. We see Piet Retief's disastrous—and fatal—mistake of attempting to make peace with the double-dealing Dingaan. We witness Zulu *impis* preparing to kill Afrikaner women and children; the Black warriors brandish their spears before helpless throngs of terrified Whites. One old woman holds a baby in the crook of her left arm while she reaches out with her right hand and grasps the muscular arm of a Zulu; she looks up at him beseechingly, but he glowers back at her with pitiless hatred. A boy tries to shield his younger sister from attack by putting his little arms over her head; another boy picks up a musket dropped by his dead father, and takes aim at his attackers, thus presaging the ultimate triumph of frontier gumption and divine will in the miraculous victory of Blood River.

The final scene in the frieze is, indeed, a depiction of this famous battle, in which the embattled Boers routed an army 20 times their size. For a people that now view themselves as outnumbered and existentially imperiled, every day losing ground to their enemies, the contemplation of such an incredible past triumph must inspire the same sort of pride and reverential longing that an observant Jew must feel when he ponders the notion of the Red Sea parting at Yahweh's command, saving the Israelites from certain doom. [67]

On Friday, December 16, 2011, I attend *Geloftedag* ceremonies at the Voortrekker Monument. It is a bright, brilliant day, and by 8 a.m., a large crowd has already gathered. Once more, as at Orania, I am struck by just how un-striking the gathered throng appears. Most are dressed in semi-formal attire, as one would for church, but many more wear jeans, shorts, and sneakers. Very few sport 19th-century period costumes, which is a bit of a disappointment. . . I'd expected to run across some colorful, brash, outspoken, feisty characters, but for the most part, this crowd just seems like a lot of orderly, peaceable, well-behaved White folks. I would almost call them *innocuous*. Aside from the penchant of many children to go barefoot (a unique Afrikaner cultural phenomenon) and the prevalence of the Afrikaans language, these people could be amiable, mild-mannered suburbanites sitting beside me at an Atlanta Braves game at Turner Field.

Still, the fact that so many of them went out of their way to attend this event must be significant, and it's quite possible that I, an *uitlander* who doesn't speak the language, am missing something. The people pack into both levels of the building, while some find shady places to sit outside; led by a keyboard player and a cantor, the crowd duly sings patriotic songs and Christmas carols from a shared program. A smiling minister delivers a sermon in a friendly, personable manner—an Afrikaner friend later tells me that he emphasized the importance of acting for the glory of God, not out of a desire for personal gain. Though this pastor related his message to the Blood River battle and its aftermath, the content of the homily still sounds like standard evangelical boilerplate, like something one might hear delivered by some blandly handsome young preacher at a Baptist megachurch in heartland America. It somehow seems like a "lite" version of Afrikanerdom, a watering down of the fierce, uncompromising spirit which built this edifice over half a century ago.

But just as I began to fret that the Boer cause may have been rendered utterly toothless by modernity, I found myself witness to a moment of real, almost elemental power, which convinced me otherwise.

Of course, this moment has to wait until all of the singing, and the speechifying, has ceased. Afterwards, the crowd gathers around a cenotaph, or plaque, located in the middle of the bottom floor. Some lean over the railing of the floor above, and peered downward. On the cenotaph reads the words "Ons vir jou, Suid-Afrika" ("We for you, South Africa").

As the noontime hour approaches, a beam of sunlight shines through a strategically carved hole high above our heads in the roof of the Monument; the crowd buzzes excitedly as the circle of sunshine makes its way along the floor, before finally alighting on the cenotaph at exactly 12:00. Then the crowd suddenly stands, and in lusty, full-throated voices, belts out "Die Stem van Suid-Afrika," the former national anthem of South Africa prior to 1994:

[69]

> *From the blue of our heaven*
> *From the depths of our sea,*
> *Over our eternal mountain ranges*
> *Where our cliffs their answer give*
>
> *We will answer to your calling,*
> *We will offer what you ask*
> *We will live, we will die,*
> *We for Thee, South Africa!*

Following this impromptu performance, the crowd gives a hearty cheer, then several parents send their children to pose in front of the sunbeam as they take photographs. People are still standing in a circle, facing one another, and I feel myself in some ways witness to a nation facing itself, wondering what comes next. It is grand and glorious to sing together, as if with one voice, of giving one's life for one's country, but what does one do when the song ends, and one recalls that his country, in essence, no longer exists?

It is a dire question that many in Europe and North America will no doubt be asking themselves in the coming years. Due to his immediate circumstances, the Afrikaner feels urgently compelled to ask it now. Whether he ultimately succeeds or fails to find the correct answer, we will find much to learn from observing the various steps he is currently taking to attempt to secure a proper homeland for himself and his children.

And if he actually manages to triumph, against all odds, and again emerges victorious, as his ancestors did at Blood River, then unreconstructed Westerners will find in the study of the Afrikaner's present struggles an invaluable treasure, an ace that we can keep in the turbulent times ahead.

LAST STAND

of the

CAPE

CRUSADERS

DEREK TURNER

The dream of
Euro-Africa
collapsed when
South African
settlers were
cast as the
world's villains.

DEREK TURNER
is Editor of the UK-based *Quarterly Review*. His articles have appeared in the *Times, Sunday Telegraph, Literary Review, Chronicles, This England*, and many other journals, and have been translated into 12 languages. His first book, a novel about immigration, *Sea Changes*, was published in 2012.

[*images*]
"Boycott-Apartheid Bus"
London, England, 1989
R Barraez D´Lucca
Creative Commons

"Euro-Africa"
Cape Town University
H. V. Morton
In Search of South Africa
(London: Methuen & Co., 1948)

"Don't be a racist

Don't be a fool!

Support black majority rule!"

The youths

repeated their slogan for about the 56th time in two minutes, this time making it even more original by using a battery-powered loudhailer. With each repetition, the members of the picket seemed to quiver with a spasm of righteous incontinence, and their fresh faces twisted in gleeful release. I felt I was witnessing some kind of therapy, as I stood below the portico 20 feet in front, trying to suppress the wide grin that their words always aroused.

The wielder of the bullhorn was a regular on the anti-Apartheid picket outside the South African embassy in Trafalgar Square, according to my colleagues a bishop's son—a fair-haired man of medium height, whose mellifluous public-school tones were evident even through the crackles and feedback of an appliance whose very nature doomed it to be the transmitter of regrettable phraseology.

Even with his artfully ripped jeans and man-of-the-people T-shirt, he was not an especially convincing tribune—but that did not really matter, because beneath the well-worn words, there lay whole continents of conviction. His was the voice of the whole world, as filtered through the opinion pages of *The Guardian*. When his eyes bored into yours, they carried a payload of wounded incomprehension.

How could *anyone* defend South Africa—how could they live with the knowledge of what they had done, were doing, to Nelson Mandela, Steve Biko, and countless other Xhosa exemplars—how could they resist the devastating logic of Paul McCartney and Stevie Wonder's "Ebony and Ivory"?

At times, his words would tumble over themselves as he tried to rush them all out, tried to be like Jesus, to drive home the message that here in the heart of London, facing Nelson's Column and the fountains in that famous Square, was a sinful stone symbol to all that was horrid. South Africa House, with its handsome colonnades and big-game carvings, a 1930s-built companion piece to the earlier Canada House opposite, was a Temple of Baal marooned by history, doomed by history, in a city and a world which had otherwise rejected (or would very soon reject) all forms of discrimination on any grounds. Afrikaner nationalists may have had a messianic mission, but clearly so did those who hated them.

The picket had been there for most of the 1980s, a near-permanent presence that had become an untidy part of the scenery—although personally I felt it detracted from rather than adorned the Neo-Classical symmetry of the Square. Although there were spasmodic demonstrations attended by hundreds, including "dignitaries" like Neil Kinnock or Joe Slovo, the picket generally occupied a 40-foot-long strip of pavement, staffed by four or five people (usually young, almost always White), demarcated by posters taped to the pavement. These earnest productions depicted scenes from Sharpeville, a sad Steve Biko behind inked-in prison bars, statistics about inequality, gnomic utterances by SS. Nelson and Marx, and anti-Conservative messages, some of which seemed to have at best a tenuous connection with the issue in hand—such as "Thatcher = Milk Snatcher" (a reference to a policy of stopping subsidized milk for Britain's schoolchildren).

[77]

Mrs. Thatcher, then still clinging to office, was hated almost as much by the protestors as the evil Afrikaners themselves. She had always opposed sanctions against South Africa, on the grounds that it was a strategically important anti-Communist power in a world still at least theoretically threatened by Bolshevism—that sanctions would not be effective—and in any case, it was up to "the market" to decide this, as everything else. Although most Conservative MPs had long since discreetly declined to go to bat for the not-very-beloved country, a diehard handful were still prepared to defend their heroine's policy in Parliament, attend embassy functions, and act as lobbyists for South African business interests.

There were always a few Metropolitan Police in attendance outside the embassy, but it was my job, as an embassy employee, to admit or reject visitors, and these included some of these MPs, along with an array of business people, expatriates seeking consular services, tourists seeking visas, and sarcastic media representatives. My colleagues and I took it in turns to monitor the visas section, the back door where the staff came and went, and the front door. As an amateur anthropologist, the latter was my favorite post, despite the demagoguery—because I could see and hear a lot of what went on among the picketers and between them and the public.

Although I always strove to look professional, I also quite enjoyed being an object of attention to the picketers, who often resorted to what they thought were winsome appeals. "You're young. What are you doing in there? You should be out here with us!" This loudspeakered line always reminded me of *The Camp of the Saints* character known as the "Panama Ranger," a young and athletic White man so-called because of the writing on his anorak, who taunts the besieged French patriots as out-of-touch elitists, and calls on them to drop their irrelevant identity and join in the anything-goes universe. Sadly, this but reinforced my vain pride in standing aloof.

These appeals were alternated with threats—"Fascist scum! Racist scum! We're going to get you!"—although the police would quickly move in to arrest these amicable animadversions. I was frequently photographed, also intended as intimidation, and perhaps some of these pictures eventually found their way into *Gay London Socialist* as "This Month's Face of Hate." That I did not wear a uniform may even have made some of the demonstrators suspect I was working for the notorious Bureau of State Security (the aptly acronymed BOSS)—but the truth was much less interesting. Out of work, I had simply walked in off the street one day when passing—more than ordinarily piqued by the picket's prosing—and asked if there were any jobs available. The head of personnel was amused and intrigued enough to admit that there was indeed a position free—and so I fell into the job, as I have fallen into most of the jobs I have ever done.

The duties were dull, although the conditions were good and my colleagues agreeable. The embassy staff's attitude towards the picketers was one of tired amusement—they simply didn't understand—and these staff members were almost all liberals, perhaps picked for this prestigious posting because of their emollient acceptability. There was an interesting cross-section of displaced Rhodesians and South Africans of assorted Afrikaans, Huguenot, English, Portuguese, and Jewish antecedents, and even some "Coloured" and black staff—a point naturally never mentioned by the demonstrators. They were uniformly clubbable and intelligent, from the ambassador down to my day-to-day colleagues, who were mostly British ex-servicemen, although there was one Afrikaner, with the stereotypical heavy jowls and drooping moustache, and a less stereotypical taste for Camus.

[79]

It was slightly surreal to be inside the handsome offices, with their fumed oak panelling and *objets d'art*, their paintings of lions in the Drakensberg or wildebeest in the Transkei, and to hear occasionally, as the traffic diminished for a moment, a faint reminder of the world's whimperers outside—". . . a-racist-don't-be-a-fool-supp. . ." before the sensible sentiments were submerged again in a blessed roar of motorbikes.

I had originally offered my services because I was irritated by the picket's one-dimensional approach to what were clearly complex questions, and the more South Africans I met, the more I knew I had been right to reject the easy answers. The South Africa displayed in the world's press was like a child's drawing—a sincere and slightly sweet cartoon in primary colours, but tending towards deficiency in the proportion and gradation departments.

There were aspects of Apartheid that sat uneasily with me, and some that seemed to make no sense—but it was obvious that things that looked one way when discussed in drawing rooms in London's more agreeable suburbs must look quite different at *veldt*-level. The salon moralizing that passed for analysis in those quarters was based on a complete lack of realism—an utter failure to understand what it must be like to be part of a small population that had from its 17th-century outset been culturally isolated, far from "home," and permanently threatened by absorption or extermination. As one of the greatest 20th-century

Afrikaner writers—incidentally no friend to Apartheid—has written "Never has such a volume of criticism been so wide of the mark."[1]

I had gradually developed a sneaking admiration for this state so lashed by the loathing of the "international community" as represented by the United Nations (ironically, Jan Smuts wrote the original Preamble to the United Nations Charter), and which was proving so resourceful in circumventing sanctions, often in alliance with Israel, that other whipping boy of the world's wiseacres. South Africa's ingenuity in everything from substitute petrol and rubber to knock-off M16s (the ordnance antithesis of the equality-evoking AK47) and selling its exports surreptitiously through an array of raffish front men and offshore operations was extraordinary. I was amused by the idea of the Black homelands, the fake countries-within-a-country with their specially-devised flags, mottos and coats of arms, their absolute monarchs and joker presidents-for-life, where nevertheless life for the ordinary people was infinitely better than anywhere else between the Limpopo and the Sahara.

[81]

I had also an appealing impression of proud Protestants, who (a little like their American equivalents) had set out into the wilderness from the Dutch East India Company's way-station, armed with little more than a gun, a Bible, and boundless courage. I knew something of the bandolier-bearing guerilla-generals, who had routed the redcoats, and their latter-day

---

[1]   W. A. de Klerk, *The Puritans in Africa: A Story of Afrikanerdom* (London: Pelican, 1975).

descendants, the SADF scouts, who, living off the land along the Angolan and Mozambiquean borders, watching always for the Cuban explosives experts, without whom Mandela's ANC would never have been able to murder anyone at all.

I had read *King Solomon's Mines*, set in a parallel Zululand, with its symbolic confrontation between the blond giant Sir Henry Curtis and black King Twala (in 1877, H. Rider Haggard personally raised the British flag over Pretoria, signaling the end of the first South African Republic) and Kipling's *Dead Drummer*, about an English country-lad named Hodge, interred far from home, whose

> *. . . landmark is a kopje-crest*
> *That breaks the veldt around;*
> *And foreign constellations west*
> *Each night above his mound.*

These and many more tumbling images fomented a yearning to see something of the bandit nation that could arouse such rhapsodizing before Apartheid was discarded, as I guessed was inevitable.

Apartheid seemed doomed to me because the array of forces ranged against it was too great, from all international institutions to deep within the supposed citadel—in Anglo-American and De Beers, in the Broederbond, and even in the Reformed Churches, separateness's supposed metaphysical motors.

It was also against the spirit of the times, the post-Holocaust, post-Age of Aquarius mood which detests on principle any exercise of naked power, or any hint of discriminating between any groups in any circumstances, unless it is to the detriment of the West. South Africans would tell me, with a knowing smile, that the Afrikaners "would never stand" for power-sharing, but it was obvious they were wrong. Bluster was not a strategy.

My ability to eavesdrop on the picket had also suggested that the arguments for Apartheid were simply not available, or if they were, only a tiny minority was willing to deploy them. Many people, not always South Africans, stopped to argue against the picket, and I had noticed that they often lost. The only times the picket was seriously disconcerted was on the very rare occasions when drunken rugby or football fans surged through and ran them down, or when they were physically attacked by supporters of John Tyndall's British National Party—but these were either apolitical or actually counter-productive incidents, only perpetuating the picketers' self-image as martyrs to "the Establishment."

[83]

Would-be defenders usually started with some variation on the theme that this wasn't about race, *but.* . . And yet Apartheid was manifestly about race, as that slippery concept was (mis)interpreted by Calvinist theologians—"the politics of redemption trying to reach down to man's existential roots."[2]

---

[2] *Ibid.*

Then they would deny that it was unjust and arbitrary, and yet clearly there were injustices and anomalies (as there are in all political systems). Then they would be called elitists, and then racists and fascists, and they would say no, but. . .

From then on, they slunk from one position to another and then another further back, until eventually they would beat a retreat much less dignified than those of their lustier forebears. A few, more intellectually honest or perhaps just more craven, would even sign the petition they had stopped to ridicule. When they had gone, the picketers would often smirk hatefully between themselves, and metaphorically preen themselves on their superior intelligence, compassion, and courage.

[84]

I occasionally confronted the activists when off duty; I found it relatively easy to face them down simply by refusing to apologize for anything, and by knowing a little history. When they would allude (as they liked to do) to the Edenic ethnic harmony that had prevailed prior to the advent of evil Europeans, I was able to cite the likes of *Mfecane* ("The Crushing") by means of which the Zulus obtained the overlordship of the Bantu in the early 19th century, and this sort of anecdote had a similarly crushing effect on their argument. Then, of course, for anyone who read the papers, there were always plenty of examples of Black African leaders behaving far, far worse towards their ostensible brethren—which is why so many of those selfsame brethren were clamouring at South Africa's borders for admittance. On one occasion, I even got several picketers to agree with me, and one of the (exceedingly rare) Black attendees followed me down to Charing Cross station specifically to shake my hand and have a rational conversation away from the gaze of his comrades-in-outrage. It was admittedly poor sport, but I felt it a kind of duty.

Fast forward a year or two, and although I had long since parted company from the embassy after the dullness became insupportable, one day I woke to find myself in a large and expensive house in Cape Town, high above the city in one of its most exclusive southern suburbs.

In the mornings, the air was cool and there were stupendous views down over the bay and, from certain places, up to Table Mountain. The quiet lane outside had a semi-rural feel, its high hedges heavy with outré blooms and haunted by large and interesting insects. It was a place of dog walkers and leotarded joggers who smiled "Good morning!" and seemed to mean it, and purring new Mercedes in whose perfect sides I could see my deeply tanned reflection. The drivers were Rand multi-millionaires and lived in new and spotless open-plan accommodation furnished from Biggie Best, with always-on air conditioning, rarely-entered libraries full of new books and much-used *braai* areas and swimming pools. There would be several such vehicles in each of the long driveways, one or maybe more than one for each inhabitant over the age of 16.

It was an apparently charmed existence for the residents, close but not too close to people of similar tastes, near to the "in"

[85]

shops and restaurants, and all around the great gorgeousness of the Western Cape. Table Mountain, the Lion's Peak, and Signal Hill overtopped an epic-scale panorama. There was Table Bay, where the high-adventuring Antonio de Saldanha had dropped anchor in 1503—False Bay, whose name hints at the dangers and heartbreak faced by such as Saldanha, down here at the Cabo das Tormentas ("Cape of Storms"), which Luís de Camões imagined as menaced by the Titan Adamastor, wind god of the Indian Ocean[3]—and Hout Bay, where baboons picked along the road and I found a 60-foot-long whale shark washed up in a cove.

Inland could be seen heaped-up azure hills, penetrated by predestined pilgrims and prospectors in search of the legendary Kingdom of Monomotapa or the golden city of Vigiti Magna. Not far away was the wine district of Stellenbosch, with its lovely and commodious Cape Dutch farmhouses festooned and swagged with vines, admired by John Ruskin and Cecil Rhodes, whose monument at Devil's Peak faces the illimitable north he never quite subdued, in a country lesser successors lost.

Keeping going along the Garden Route, you came to the Klein Karoo—a quietly keening mini-desert where the wind rolled the red sand over low flowers so bright as to look like they were

---

[3]   "Even as I spoke, an immense shape / Materialized in the night air, / Grotesque, and of enormous stature, / With heavy jowls, and an unkempt beard, / Scowling from shrunken, hollow eyes, / Its complexion earthy and pale, / Its hair grizzled and matted with clay, / Its mouth coal black, teeth yellow with decay." *Lusiads*, Canto Five (first published 1572, my edition 1997, tr. Landeg White).

made of plastic, towards Oudtshoorn, probably the only town in the world devoted to ostriches. Then the Route brought you back down to Plettenberg Bay, where the Atlantic starts to think about becoming the Indian Ocean and you were acutely aware the seaways carried not just whale sharks but also great whites and that there was nothing else whatever between you and Antarctica.

There was the little trading port of Knysna, founded by one George Rex from Whitechapel—what a contrast!—with its semi-legendary forest elephants, the world's southernmost population, which romancers averred with understandable untruth still stalked its most secluded glades.

Back among the Anglos in Cape Town, cicadas itched and whirred in all the acres of gardens, also graced by fireflies that performed intricate electric ballets in the warm blackness beneath the pruned shrubs—command performances for the laughing, drinking, gossiping groups lolling on the perfect lawns their hard work had purchased. They were the Cape's economic and therefore social elite—a racial elite, too, in those dog days of Apartheid, passing Indian summers just before the end of the White order.

[87]

But then there were the omnipresent Others—those strangers who were always there like shadows, doing the hands-on work of tending those lawns until they looked like something from a home improvement magazine, clearing up all the dishes and glasses left behind by the late-night revelers, polishing those multiple Mercedes, dusting those Biggie Best knick-knacks, dandling the flaxen infants, cleaning out the toilets, taking away the tarantulas. It was not, of course, Apartheid at all, I soon noticed, but part-Apartheid, in which one side wanted to have their racial cake and eat it too, enjoying simultaneously the undeserved pampering and the feeling of socio-moral superiority over the allegedly more proletarian Afrikaners. Excellent meals were cooked and cleared away, sparkling glasses tinkled and were taken, and swimming pools were raked free of leaves, all by semi-invisibles who were simply assumed to be inferiors (without that ever actually being said).

[88] Cape Town liberal sentiment (and everyone here was liberal) did not like to dwell on the subject, but the fact was that the haves were (ahem!) White and the have-nots were (ahem!) Black. The economic and social distance between both peoples was stupendous—even more so here among the ashamed Anglophone millionaires than in the most *verkrampte* up-country dorp, where (according to cliché) large meaty Boers wearing khaki shorts rampaged constantly through peaceful suburbs wielding *sjamboks*.

Mandela was still on Robben Island, a princeling prisoner of conscience who gracefully received gushing embassies and editorialists from abroad. Most of the residents of the suburb appeared to vote for the Progressive Federal Party, and some knew Helen Suzman and Harry Schwarz socially. Power sharing was in the air everywhere, and everyone who was anyone wanted it, and soon, very soon—but not just yet. It was inevitable, desirable, but the trouble was that there would need to be education first—a lot of education—because you see, Derek, the Blacks have been so long oppressed that they can't do the simplest thing properly—the poor pets just need leadership for a little longer. That was what those frightful Dutchmen didn't understand, with their funny Old Testament fervor, their phobias and provincialism, their bad table manners and appalling dress sense—they were haters, whereas we are (sigh!) reluctant realists. At the back of some minds even then there may have been a comforting (if unconfessed) awareness that if the coming new country became uncongenial, there was always that second passport in the antique bureau.

There were several prize exhibits to prove how more [89] advanced the Capetonians were over their embarrassing co-Europeans. There was Desmond Tutu, the Black Anglican Archbishop of Cape Town, who harangued the government every week from his ornate pulpit and in local newspaper columns. There were the Cape Coloureds, who held a strange intermediate place in the hierarchy between the Whites and their darker-skinned "brothers." There were wealthy Indian entrepreneurs and conversely poor Whites, fixers of *bakkies*, and proprietors of suburban bottle shops—some of whom were, as the local saying went, "a waste of a white skin."

Everyone lucky enough to live in the suburb was kind and considerate to their Black employees—ostentatiously so, even embarrassingly so. From the "maids" (most of whom had probably lost that status *aetatis* 14) to the "garden boys" (many of whom had grey hair), they were constantly talked to, and talked down to—empathized with and ordered around. Their pay was good, their holiday requests were usually granted, their ailments and families anxiously enquired after—but employer and staff never sat at the same table and at the end of each day, the staff would say in their clipped voices "Goodnight, Sir" or "Goodnight, Midim" to Whites often less likeable than themselves, and waft down the hill to heaving hovels in Khayelitsha, never to see each other again until work began the following morning. The suburbanites themselves obviously felt unsure having staff, and this was probably a function of social insecurity as much as racial, because so many here were self-made, enriched by government contracts necessitated by the years of sanctions.

[90]

They had reason to feel insecure. Part-Apartheid, with its cumbersome procedures and army of functionaries, brought the races just close enough to breed black resentment, with its daily petty insults and reminders of the contrast between black and white living conditions. Whites knew this, and this made them afraid. It was after dark you realized the essentially frightened feeling in the suburb—when you suddenly saw that all these welcoming open-plan places had high fences around them, often electrified, and burglar alarms and cameras, and warning signs about roaming Rottweilers or Rhodesian Ridgebacks. Large dogs would bark at blacks and not at whites, a fact in which the owners took shamefaced satisfaction.

Some of the houses—the largest, lived in by MPs, former Mayors and leftish media personalities—had panic buttons to the police station, their own private security guards and gun cabinets full of elegantly oiled menace. At the bottom of the garden of the house in which I was staying was an old, gloomy, high hedge of wild almond, purportedly the same one planted in 1652 by the first "Commander of the Cape," Jan van Riebeeck, to keep prowling lions and Hottentots away from his sleeping Cape Colonists. Three hundred plus years on, the colony was still sleeping uneasily, still a bridgehead on a huge and hostile continent.

One afternoon we drove, at judicial speed, through Cape Flats, the main Black township, and I was astounded by the surreal scenes—miles (no exaggeration) of fly-blown shacks and shops, thrumming shebeens, smashed-up concrete toilet blocks, burned-out cars, gaunt dogs and goats, mangy cats, drifts of bottles and excreta, and a few people lying comatose (maybe dead) in the middle of the potholed roads at midday without anyone paying any attention. All heads swivelled and appraising eyes weighed up our pale physiognomies as we motored through, feeling uncomfortably conspicuous in our skins. It looked like the worst place on earth, and I was told afterwards by a Progressive Federal Party activist that we had been crazy to essay "those awful people" without a couple of pistols. I thought of those London geniuses who had so often advised me not to be a racist, not to be a fool, and wished they could be there rather than in London.

[91]

Between the mutually fearful, unilaterally envious different planets of the Flats and Cape Town's primped suburbs, there were other anomalies and interdependencies that made Apartheid as practiced unviable. Afrikaans had borrowed words and concepts from the Bantu languages and from the indentured Malays, who were ancestors of many of the Coloureds. As in the American South, even the most theoretically racist Boer backwoodsman made exceptions for "good Blacks"—whether reliable farmhands, or historical figures like the Coloured Will Jordan, who led a hardcore of anti-British refuseniks to safety in Angola through tribal wars and the desolate landscapes of the Kaokoveld. Writing of the mid-19th century, it has been said:

> *In spite of the vast and obvious difference between Christian white and heathen black, there was much in common between the Boer farmer and the African farm labourer, and each had the leisure to adapt himself to the other's habits. The relationship between the two was patriarchal and personal.*[4]

Such understandings persist even now, with anecdotes of targeted White farmers being defended, not by the police, but by loyal Black workers. Afrikaners and Blacks are sometimes said to have more in common than Afrikaners and English-speaking Whites, between whom there was (and is) unfinished business.

----

[4]   Leo Marquard, *The Story of South Africa* (New York: Praeger, 1968).

There are entirely justifiable resentments still felt by Afrikaner nationalists—who being the descendants of Netherlandish and French Calvinist battlers against Catholic absolute monarchs have always tended towards the predestinarian and republican in their politics. Even now, they recall the gradual imperialist encroachments under the likes of the cold fish Milner, the long snubbing and suppression of Afrikaans, the atrocious treatment meted out to Afrikaner women and children in the world's first concentration camps, and several attempts to supplant Afrikaner workers in favor of cheaper Blacks by British big business (how strange to recall that in the 1920s, Afrikaner nationalists were supported by the British Labour Party).

[93]

It was such folk-memories that made even moderate nationalists like James Hertzog seek to avoid involvement in World War II (this cost him the Prime Ministership in 1939, in favor of Jan Smuts), while some—notoriously J. F. J. Van Rensburg and his paramilitary *Ossewabrandwag*—collaborated with Germany. When Eugene Terre'blanche's *Afrikaner Weerstandsbeweging* (AWB) adopted its swastika-like triskelion emblem in 1973, it was an act of provocation—but it was also an outcropping of a long tradition. That Terre'blanche could not see how counter-productive a choice this was typifies the ineptitude of his movement.

The British had introduced laws discriminating against Blacks as early as 1847, but the post-1948 Apartheid settlement was unique in its thoroughness. The unionists and moderate nationalists who had brought South Africa into the war were swept suddenly out of office and even out of public culture, in favour of a new coterie of radical intellectuals who fused existential fears about the brooding non-White majority with anti-British sentiment, republicanism, romantic nationalism, and an eschatology which stressed man's "total depravity" and Afrikanerdom's special place in God's affections. "Christian-national" thinkers like N. Diederichs, P. J. Mayer, and G. Cronjé exerted much influence over politicians like Vorster, Malan, and Verwoerd (the latter himself a considerable theorist), and between 1948 and the early 1970s, over 200 separate Apartheid laws were passed, governing almost every aspect of co-existence. In *Religion and the Rise of Capitalism*, R. H. Tawney had complained of Calvin that he had made Geneva "a city of glass, in which every household lived its life under the supervision of spiritual police"—and something of this snooping spirit pervaded South Africa. Balthazar Vorster, Prime Minister between 1966 and 1974, used to joke to those visiting the country for the first time, "Welcome to the happiest police state in the world."

[94]

But Apartheid was also informed by a Christian concern for social justice—as Verwoerd believed, it was "designed for happiness." The framework was devised to preserve White supremacy—but also to allow all groups to create their own future with generous assistance from the Europeans. There was also a fully functioning legal system which often successfully opposed the government.

Proclaimed in 1961, the new Republic was full of the practical spirit of Piet Retief, one of the leaders of the Great Trek. Retief's manifesto of February 1837 is notable for its dearth of abstractions. It is altogether of a different order from the American Declaration of Independence, which, of course, had been produced by people of similar religious outlook and in a similar political position. The difference is that whereas the Founding Fathers had been exposed to the Enlightenment, most Afrikaners had left Europe too early.

Retief's solitary concession to newly-fashionable nostrums of "inalienable" rights is a pledge to "uphold the just principles of liberty," but as de Klerk observes, this "is still an *obiter dictum*" in a document that merely lists grievances and proffers a single remedy—Exodus from the City of Destruction in quest of Zion. The manifesto incorporates the unvarnished essence of the Apartheid we in the West came to know and were told we must hate:

[95]

> *[W]hilst we will take care that no-one shall be held in a state of slavery, it is our determination to maintain such regulations as may suppress crime, and preserve proper relations between master and servant.*

To Retief's *Voortrekkers*, race differences were "natural distinctions" and to say otherwise was "contrary to the laws of God."[5] In the frontier circumstances, it was

---

[5]   Anna Steenkamp, a niece of Piet Retief, cited in de Klerk, *The Puritans in Africa.*

hardly surprising that there should have been racial distrust; Retief himself was murdered in 1838 on the orders of the Zulu king Dingane, unarmed while attending a party at Dingane's *kraal*. But that there had always been this physical as well as social dichotomy lent indignant impetus to the later global campaign to end all distinctions between master and servant, Black and White, even male and female—and not just in South Africa, but everywhere White Westerners are extreme enough to want to exist.

As the 1960s rolled into the 1970s, Afrikaners found it increasingly difficult to justify Apartheid to outsiders. There were a few external outposts of understanding, like Holland, with its familial connections and where a minority of the population remains conservative and Calvinist. The Afrikaners also found support amongst Ulster's Protestants, who saw their minority status in a Catholic majority island as being analogous to that of the Afrikaners in a Black-majority continent—and, of course, among Israelis, appreciative of Afrikaner philo-Semitism and alert to tactical exigencies.

But the rest of the outside world had by now developed its own kind of intransigence, just as the Afrikaners were starting to lose theirs through a combination of business boycotts, cultural and sporting sanctions and constant calumniation. Small pieces of Apartheid legislation were allowed to slide into disuse, and the government spent countless millions of Rand on public relations exercises, but this, of course, encouraged rather than sated the prowling PC predators.

Then the downfall of the Soviet Union removed the last strategic reason for American support (which had in any case been grudging and furtive), and the ejection of Mrs. Thatcher from office the following year finally knocked Britain out of the geopolitical game. F. W. de Klerk was an executor rather than an instigator; if it had not been him, it would have been another second-rate politician from a reassuringly conventional Afrikaner background. In 1994, the world had its way, and White voters voted two to one in favour of power-sharing. The compromise *Prinsevlag* of 1928—with its remembrances of the House of Orange and Van Riebeeck, and its clumsily-contained Union, Orange Free State, and Transvaal emblems—was hauled down in favour of the vibrant Y-fronts which we in the West have come to know and are told we must love. The Y-fronts themselves were intended as an interim flag, and barely got approval in time for their first hoisting—a hint, perhaps, of disunity to come.

[97]

Gallant writers (always too few), like Dan Roodt, Philip du Toit, and Ilana Mercer, have written powerfully of what has happened since—the increasing inefficiency and corruption of government, the decline in public health, the coarsening of culture, the humiliations visited upon the former masters by the former servants, the symbolic renaming of landmarks—the carjackings, the robberies, the rapes, the drive-by shootings, and, most symbolically of all, the farm murders. The proud pioneers who persuaded the deserts to bloom and made their homes at the end of long roads in lonely places where they might be free and near to God are being picked off one by one, farm by farm, and dorp by dorp—and they are now recoiling from the land that they made their own with all good intentions, and thought they might keep. Their houses are starting to slide back into the reddish earth, their carefully demarcated fields reverting to scrub, their intricate irrigation systems seizing up as surely as the eccentric, execrated worldview that allowed them to be installed. Gradually, through a combination of political paralysis, socioeconomic sclerosis, cultural cleansing, and fatal *force majeure*, Boers are being beaten back towards the coasts, crushed more slowly but just as surely as Zulus once crushed Bantu.

The consequences for South Africa's particular brand of civilization are clearly extremely ominous, but it is less frequently recognized that the implications for non-Afrikaners are also enormous. The eyeless, instinctive forces presently pushing Whites off the veldt will not halt at the edges of the cities—indeed, they are already at work within the cities. Nor do they generally trouble to distinguish between angry Afrikaner nationalist and angst-ridden Anglophone abstractionist—they possess a logic and momentum of their own, and care no more for the airy dews of Eurocentric liberalism than they do for the refinements of Reformed eschatology or Biggie Best wallpaper patterns.

Even in the shiny, celebrated "new" South Africa, sheer strength rules much as it always has—pushing urgently into all newly vacated spaces, sweeping aside unaffordable knick-knack considerations in order to gratify more elemental emotions. Whether they knew it or not, the concerned Capetonians and reckless ranters of Trafalgar Square were alike conduits of chaos, condemning thousands to deletion to soothe their own exquisite sensibilities. Not content with this success, a few of these lounge Lenins are even now attempting to assure Afrikanerdom's extirpation—while yet others have turned their troubled thoughts to ways in which they can most effectually undermine other outcrops of the wicked West.

What next for Afrikaners, as the Malans and Verwoerds vanish from the map and the imagination? Many have already outspanned overseas—strangely enough, often those who decided not to be racists, not to be fools, and so voted for power-sharing. But many others have nowhere to go or cannot afford to leave, and must take their chances in a country which has already changed hugely and will every year become less familiar and less safe.

[99]

It is impossible for Afrikaners to "take back" their country, even if it were desirable—that belonged to another, unrecoverable age. They must for the foreseeable future exist on sufferance, playing a loaded game by alien rules, swimming in an ocean of Others who have reason to resent them. For the foreseeable future, they are constrained to do what persecuted peoples have always done in evil times—inspan into Bantustans of their own, look in on themselves and heal their hurts, tend the groves and mend the walls, teach the children and make plans. But howsoever hurt, they still have strengths—their tried and tested faith, their cultural identity, their shared history, their close links to the landscape—and inside the timidest heart subsists something of the psalm-singing corduroy commandos who once set the world at defiance, and may one day ride again.   ৵►

The

GEOPOLITICS

of

WHITE
DISPOSSESSION

K.R. BOLTON

*Beyond demographics
and political
correctness, the
destruction of White
rule in Africa was
part of a grand
strategy of financial
domination.*

K. R. BOLTON
holds doctorates in historical
theology and theology. He is
a contributing writer for *The
Foreign Policy Journal,* and a
Fellow of the Academy of Social
and Political Research in Greece.
His papers and articles have been
published by both scholarly
and popular media, including
the *International Journal of
Social Economics, Journal of
Social, Political, and Economic
Studies, Geopolitika, World
Affairs, India Quarterly,* and *The
Initiate: Journal of Traditional
Studies.* His most recent book
is *Revolution From Above:
Manufacturing 'Dissent' in the
New World Order.*

[*image*]
"The World is Not Enough"
The Great Dictator *(1940)*
Charlie Chaplin
United Artists
Wikimedia

The story of the eclipse of White rule in Africa, as with the European colonies of Indochina and elsewhere, is one of calculated power-politics on a global scale. To understand it, one must look beyond the vicissitudes of Apartheid, Nelson Mandela, and political correctness, as well as the debates that raged in the American media over economic sanctions of South Africa. Those who brought ruin to White Africa were not, as is commonly supposed among conservatives, Moscow-trained Communists and terrorists; it was, instead, the "Money Power" centered in Washington and New York. And the story begins long before the period of decolonization.

The Congress of Berlin of 1884-1885, which was called in an effort to regulate the colonization of Africa, marked, perhaps, the last time Europe acted collectively *vis-à-vis* non-Europeans in support of White interests (and unencumbered by Liberal etiolation.) The Congress brought the European colonial powers together to delineate spheres of interest and allow the harmonious development of the Continent.[1] (The U.S. was also a signatory, showing that it had wider interests in the world than suggested by the Monroe Doctrine.)

A mere 35 years later, so much had changed. In a speech before Congress in 1918, President Woodrow Wilson laid out his vision for the reconstitution of the world in the aftermath of the Great War, his "Fourteen Points."[2] Wilson articulated a self-consciously *globalist* mindset—and one that sounded the death knell of White rule.

In making his declaration, Wilson's audiences were, first, the precarious Bolshevik regime[3] and, second, the colonial peoples. Wilson presented himself and the United States of America as the leaders of "anti-imperialism." The new international order Wilson outlined was based on global free-trade that would necessitate the elimination of imperial barriers. The "Fourteen Points" include:

---

[1] Congress of Berlin, http://courses.wcupa.edu/jones/his312/misc/berlin.htm (accessed May 1, 2012).

[2] Woodrow Wilson, "Fourteen Points," 1918, http://www.fordham.edu/halsall/mod/1918wilson.html (accessed May 1, 2012).

[3] The "intervention" in Russia by U.S. troops supposedly to help the White armies against the Bolsheviks is a historical myth. See: K R Bolton, *Revolution from Above* (London: Arktos Media Ltd., 211), 66-97.

III. The removal, so far as possible, of all economic barriers and the establishment of an equality of trade conditions among all the nations consenting to the peace and associating themselves for its maintenance.

V. A free, open-minded, and absolutely impartial adjustment of all colonial claims, based upon a strict observance of the principle that in determining all such questions of sovereignty the interests of the populations concerned must have equal weight with the equitable claims of the government whose title is to be determined.

XIV. A general association of nations must be formed under specific covenants for the purpose of affording mutual guarantees of political independence and territorial integrity to great and small states alike.[4]

[105]

Though Wilson referenced the Central Powers (America's enemy in the Great War), the "Fourteen Points" were ultimately about the reorganization of the entire world, and they are unequivocally directed against *all* empires:

In regard to these essential rectifications of wrong and assertions of right we feel ourselves to be intimate partners of all the governments and peoples associated together against the Imperialists. We cannot be separated in interest or divided in purpose. We stand together until the end.[5]

---

[4] Woodrow Wilson, "Fourteen Points."

[5] *Ibid.*

Wilson's declaration gave the non-White, colonized peoples the assurance of America's support.

Wilson's call for non-White empowerment, as much as the debacle of the Great War itself, demonstrated to the "colored world" the weaknesses of Europeans. On this matter, Oswald Spengler wrote poignantly:

> *This war was a defeat of the white races, and the Peace of 1918 was the first great triumph of the coloured world: symbolised by the fact that today it is allowed to have a say in the disputes of the white states among themselves in the Geneva League of Nations—which is nothing but a miserable symbol of shameful things.*[6]

[106]

Wilson's doctrine has remained the basis of U.S. policy. His message was both pro-Bolshevik (with the call for the end of empires) and made on behalf of financial interests (with his call for the establishment of global markets). This Moscow-Wall Street paradox resolves when one remembers that a segment of the latter— led by Jacob Schiff, of Kuhn, Loeb & Company, and Paul Warburg— had actually financed Lenin and the Bolshevik Revolution.

THE ANGLO-AMERICAN BREACH

Many on the American Right have fantasized that there was an alliance between British imperialists, from the old Cecil

---

[6] O. Spengler, *The Hour of Decision* (New York: Alfred A Knopf, 1934), 209.

Rhodes Round Table network, and the internationalists, centered around Wilson and the burgeoning Council on Foreign Relations (CFR).[7]

The truth is quite the opposite. When the empires became too restrictive for high finance, an anti-imperialist, internationalist agenda, centered in Washington and New York, became the new paradigm. In fact, the British imperialists, of the Round Table Group, and the Wall Street internationalists, represented by Col. Edward House's think-tank The Inquiry,[8] fell out with one another over aims for the post-war order. Some internationalist bankers, industrialists, and intellectuals had intended to unite with the British Round Table Group, with the aim of creating an "American Institute of International Affairs." However, it soon transpired that neither the British nor the

[107]

---

[7]   This misconception came from a conspiratorial rendering of several dozen pages from American historian Dr. Carroll Quigley's *Tragedy and Hope*. Quigley, however, got the facts uncharacteristically wrong, and his book has since spawned a great deal of misleading theorizing. Thom Burnett explains that the identification of what Quigley, (and subsequent conspiracy writers) call an "Anglophile" network for world domination is a misinterpretation. (See W. Cleon Skousen, *The Naked Capitalist: A Review and Commentary on Dr Carroll Quigley's book* Tragedy and Hope (Salt Lake City: privately printed, 1971).)

[8]   After World War I, The Inquiry became the Council on Foreign Relations, originating for the purposes of advising President Wilson on post-War foreign policy. See: K.R. Bolton, *Revolution from Above*, 30-47.

Americans were eager to continue with such a joint project.[9]

The journalist Thom Burnett[10] has shown that after the Second World War, the globalists around the CFR were eager to co-operate with the USSR in establishing a post-war New World Order—but would concede nothing to British imperial interests. These American-based plutocrats, working along the same anti-imperial direction as the USSR, sought to undermine and replace the British and all other European empires. U.S.-Soviet post-war co-operation was, however, rejected by Moscow, despite Washington's many overtures.[11]

[108]

THE ATLANTIC CHARTER

---

[9]   Peter Grose confirms this early Anglo-U.S. breach in the official CFR history: To Whitney Shepardson fell the task of informing the British colleagues of this unfortunate reality. Crossing to London, he recalled thinking that 'it might be quite unpleasant to have to say for the first time that the Paris Group of British colleagues could not be members' of the American branch. The explanation to the British was begun (shall we say?) haltingly. However, instead of the frigid look which had been feared, the faces of the British governing body showed slightly red and very happy. They had reached the same conclusion in reverse, but had not yet found a good way of getting word to the other side of the Atlantic!' See P. Grose, *Continuing The Inquiry: The Council on Foreign Relations from 1921 to 1996* (New York: Council on Foreign Relations, 2006). The entire book can be read online at: Council on Foreign Relations, http://www.cfr.org/about/history/cfr/index.html (accessed May 1, 2012).

[10]   Thom Burnett and Alex Games, *Who Really Runs the World?* (London: Collins and Brown, 2005), 102.

[11]   See K.R. Bolton, *Revolution from Above*, 24-25.

The Second World War had brought the European empires to exhaustion, and the U.S. and the USSR emerged as the dominant powers in the midst of European ruin.

The *Atlantic Charter*, drafted while the war was still ongoing in 1941, established the U.S. vision for the post-World War II era; the document expresses the same internationalist, anti-imperial agenda as the Wilsonian manifesto. Point Three of the Charter states that the U.S. and Britain guaranteed to "respect the right of all peoples to choose the form of government under which they will live." As with the "Fourteen Points," the focus for the postwar era was on international free trade, which would intrinsically undermine imperial preferences. Point Four stated that Britain and the U.S. would

[109]

> *endeavor, with due respect for their existing obligations, to further the enjoyment by all States, great or small, victor or vanquished, of access, on equal terms, to the trade and to the raw materials of the world which are needed for their economic prosperity.*[12]

Churchill was alarmed by Roosevelt's intentions, as was evident in the account of proceedings given by the President's son, Elliott. Washington's postwar agenda would be the dismantling of the empires for the purpose of establishing American supremacy under the guise of free trade. Roosevelt

---

[12]   Franklin D. Roosevelt and Winston S. Churchill, *The Atlantic Charter*, 14 August 1941, accessed May 1, 2012, http://usinfo.org/docs/democracy/53.htm..

said to Churchill:

> *Of course, after the war, one of the preconditions of any lasting peace will have to be the greatest possible freedom of trade. No artificial barriers. As few favoured economic agreements as possible. Opportunities for expansion. Markets open for healthy competition.*[13]

When Churchill raised the question of the Empire's trade agreements, Roosevelt interjected:

> *Those Empire trade agreements are a case in point.... The peace cannot include any continued despotism. The structure of the peace demands and will get equality of peoples. Equality of peoples involves the utmost freedom of competitive trade. Will anyone suggest that Germany's attempt to dominate trade in central Europe was not a major contributing factor to war?*[14]

Note that Roosevelt states that a major factor in the war against Germany was the Reich's success in negotiating what was becoming a self-sufficient trading bloc based on barter, thereby taking states out of the international trade and financial system. Roosevelt aimed for international domination by the elimination, not only of the Reich, but of all the Allied Empires, which he, more or less, equated with the German system.

[110]

---

[13] Elliott Roosevelt, *As He Saw It* (New York: Duell, Sloan and Pearce, 1946), 35.

[14] *Ibid.*

The following day, Churchill spoke in despair, knowing that Britain could not survive the war without U.S. support: "'Mr. President, I believe you are trying to do away with the British Empire. Every idea you entertain about the structure of the post-war world demonstrates it.'"[15]

Churchill was quite correct.

THE COLD WAR

The Roosevelt policy makes clear that Washington aimed to achieve global hegemony via free trade on the ruins of the European empires. In place of these empires, there was to emerge a United Nations World Government, which would operate as a façade for U.S. plutocracy. The plan was based on two planks:

[111]

[1]   Vesting nominal authority in the UN General Assembly, which would function as a world parliament on the basis of majority vote. Decolonization would mean that votes would be packed in favor of the U.S., which would easily buy off the new states.

[2]   So-called "internationalization" of atomic energy through the UN Atomic Energy Agency,

---

[15] *Ibid.,* 31.

under the terms of the "Baruch Plan" (1946), which, again, would mean *de facto* control by the U.S.

The USSR would be expected to be a junior partner—but it rebuffed the U.S. agenda and stymied the desired world state. The result was the Cold War and heated anti-Soviet rhetoric throughout the United States, which replaced the pro-Soviet propaganda that had been prominent during the war. Andrei Gromyko, Moscow's Foreign Minster, reminisced decades later that the USSR explicitly regarded the U.S. plans for the UN and the "Baruch Plan" as the means by which the USA would dominate the world and that both were rejected by Moscow as such.[16]

[112]

The bogeyman of world Communism provided a valuable pretext for the U.S. to extend its hegemony over the world, under the guises of "protection from Communism" and advancing "freedom." (Today, "regime change," "democratization," and "development" are the catchwords of choice.) Such was the policy pursued in Africa at the expense of European rule.

THE DECOLONIZATION OF AFRICA

While Washington pursued its decolonization agenda, the White peoples of Africa simply became collateral damage— the targets Mau Mau in Kenya, Holden Roberto's butchers in

---

[16] See K.R. Bolton, "Origins of the Cold War and how Stalin Foiled a New World Order," *Foreign Policy Journal*, May 31, 2010, accessed May 1, 2012, http://www.foreignpolicyjournal.com/2010/05/31/origins-of-the-cold-war-how-stalin-foild-a-new-world-order/.

Angola, and the thugs who hold sway today in former-Rhodesia and South Africa. Washington not only left the Whites to their fate but actually empowered their Black enemies and usurpers.

Conservatives throughout the West often looked with alarm at the prospect of the USSR controlling the former African colonies, and their vast mineral wealth. But the Communist Menace functioned mostly as misdirection, as Washington advanced *its* agenda of deconstructing European empires and promoting its Black minions.

While the USSR trained Black leaders at Patrice Lumumba University[17], the U.S. was training and funding its own Black cadres to man puppet governments.

[113]

The first imperial powers to be targeted by the USA were France and Britain in West Africa. Washington dolled out $94.7 million to West Africa, with the intent of displacing European administrations. In 1955, The U.S. House of Representatives stated, "the United States should administer its foreign policies and programs and exercise its influence so as to support other peoples in their efforts to achieve self-government or independence."[18]

---

[17] Clara Germani, "Moscow's academic nightmare, University in decline: Patrice Lumumba University," *The Baltimore Sun*, 5 November 1995, accessed May 1, 2012, http://articles.baltimoresun.com/1995-11-05/news/1995309007_1_patrice-lumumba-dream-school-moscow.

[18] Frederick Pedler, *Main Currents of West African History*, 1940-1978 (New York: Barnes & Noble, 1979), 96, 267.

In 1953, the Africa-America Institute (AAI) was established to fund and train the Black leadership cadre of decolonized Africa. The stated purpose was to enable the U.S. to "build relationships with the new African leadership," as the White administrators were ousted. Debbie Meyer, an AAI director, stated that over the course of 50 years, 22,000 Africans have received their postgraduate education in the United States, many having returned to Africa "to play leading roles in developing their countries and in *linking them to the global economy*" (emphasis added).[19]

The stated aim of the U.S. has not changed since President Wilson: to establish a world order based on a single economic paradigm, that of the free market and the international finance system upon which it is hinged.

Among AAI's first major programs was the establishment of the "U.S.-South Africa Leader Exchange Program" in 1958.[20] The AAI's Guinea Scholarship Program (1960-1969) provided the training for the new leadership of "post-independence Guinea," with funding from the American government agency USAID.[21] The Southern African Student Program (1961-1983) was funded by the

---

[19]   The Africa-America Institute, 'about AAI', accessed May 1, 2012, http://www.aaionline.org/about-aai/."

[20]   The Africa-America Institute, "History," accessed May 1, 2012, http://www.aaionline.org/about-aai/history/1950s/.

[21]   The Africa-America Institute, accessed May 1, 2012, http://www.aaionline.org/programs/past-programs/the-guinea-scholarship-program-gsp-1960-%E2%80%93-1969/.

U.S. State Department, as "an effort to provide educational training to students from South Africa, Namibia, Angola, Mozambique, and Zimbabwe, to provide a cadre of leadership in these countries which were transitioning into independent nations."[22] The African Training Program (1964-1969) was directed toward Africans in the French colonies, also with funding from USAID.

In 1975, a year following the Portuguese abandonment of its territories, the AAI established the Development Training Program for Portuguese-Speaking Africa (DTPSA) to establish the post-colonial leadership for the former colonies of Angola, Mozambique, Guinea-Bissau, Cape Verde, and São Tome and Principe, once again with funding from USAID.[23]

[115]

The Portuguese had been tough to crack, and the regular army had uprooted the Black Liberation Front of Mozambique (FRELIMO) in 1970 with Operation Gordian Knot. At the time, FRELIMO was receiving largess from the Ford Foundation via the Mozambique Institute[24], so the Portuguese soldiers were up against much more than jungle guerrillas.

---

[22] The Africa-America Institute, accessed May 1, 2012, http://www. aaionline.org/programs/past-programs/southern-african-student-program-sasp-1961-%E2%80%93-1983/.

[23] The Africa-America Institute, accessed May 1, 2012, http://www. aaionline.org/programs/past-programs/development-training-program-for-portuguese-speaking-africa-dtpsa-1975-%E2%80%93-1985/.

[24] B Whitaker, *The Foundations: An Anatomy of Philanthropy and Society* (London: Eyre Methuen, 1974), 24.

Portugal had been able to hold Africa for so long because the Portuguese state (the Estado Novo, led for decades by António de Oliveira Salazar) had established a unique social order. The government functioned on Catholic, corporatist, and nationalist principles; it was thus one of the few states in the world that could not be controlled by international finance. Ivor Benson, who lived in Africa and knew the situation intimately, having been an adviser to the Rhodesian Government, remarked, "in Portugal, politics has remained in power and has not become subordinate to economics. . . . [T]hey have not made the Gross National Product their God. Therefore in Portugal economics is the servant, not the master."[25]

[116]

Moreover, the Portuguese leaders recognized that they faced more than Communist terrorists. Dr. Franco Noguieira, Portugal's Foreign Minister, exposed the forces at work in Africa, stating:

> Africa has been subjected to a regime that excludes European interests and African interests as well, neither being sufficiently strong to impose themselves. A form of autonomy and independence has been created which ensures the destruction of the old forms of sovereignty and permits the setting up of new forms of sovereignty so precarious and so artificial that it is an easy matter to dominate them. The result has been that the real autonomy and the real control are to be found outside the frontiers of the new political units. The aim is to

---

[25] I. Benson, *This Worldwide Conspiracy* (Melbourne: New Times Ltd., 1972), 73.

dominate Angola and Mozambique and to include them in the spheres of foreign influences, to utilise their economic and strategic positions for the benefit of other Powers.[26]

Fernando Andresen Guimarães, of the UN Department for Peacekeeping Operations, stated that the U.S. gave support at an early stage to the murderous Holden Roberto of National Liberation Front of Angola (FNLA), Washington's favored revolutionary army within the Portuguese Empire:

The Kennedy administration also acted beyond the United Nations and sought directly to support an anti-colonial movement against the Portuguese. Holden Roberto, the UPA [Union of Peoples of Angola] (and later FNLA leader) had by the end of the 1950s established a wide range of contacts in the United States. Due to its prominent role in the anti-colonial uprising in northern Angola in 1961, the UPA was the Angolan nationalist movement with the most international exposure. Washington authorized the CIA to extend support to Roberto and UPA.[27]

[117]

In 1959, Roberto traveled to Washington, where he met Kennedy and expressed his appreciation of U.S. support:

A university scholarship programme had been

---

[26] Quoted by Benson, *This Worldwide Conspiracy*, 70-73.

[27] F. A. Guimarães, "The United State and Decolonisation of Angola" paper presented at Portugal, a Europa e os Estados Unidos da América, Lisbon, October 2003, accessed May 1, 2012, http://www.ipri.pt/artigos/artigo.php?ida=5.

established for African students from the Portuguese colonies; the military assistance programme for Portugal was cut back from the original US$ 25 million to US$ 3 million; a ban on commercial sales of arms to Portugal was imposed in mid-1961; and the US supported the prohibition on the use of NATO war matériel in Africa.[28]

Roberto had also been on a $10,000-a-year retainer from the CIA.[29]

As Portugal's colonial conflicts began to metastasize into the "Overseas War" (as it was known), with resulting inscription and massive expenditures, the government of Marcelo Caetano (Salazar's successor) became increasingly unpopular with the Portuguese public. The regime eventually fell in 1974, through a *coup* by leftist junior army officers, who soon after fully dismantled the Portuguese Empire.

Kicking Portugal out of Africa was just the first step for the Money Power and its allied organizations. In Africa, the AAI operated training programs for "refugees" (presumably fleeing terrorists) including the East Africa Refugee Program (1962-1971) and the Southern African Training Program (1971-1976). The initial program was for the training of personnel "in anticipation of independence." The latter program—once Portugal had abandoned Africa—was then directed towards the remaining White states of Southern Africa: "Namibia, South Africa and Zimbabwe, for employment in their countries of

---

[28]   F.A. Guimarães, *ibid.*

[29]   *New York Times*, September 25, 1975.

asylum with a later focus on the repatriation of trainees." This program was continued through 1976-1981, as usual, with funding from USAID.[30]

After the Portuguese had fled Mozambique, the Money Power moved in, unperturbed by noises about "nationalization" by their Black surrogates. Millions in aid money poured in from the West, and the very day that new President Samora Machel announced his nationalization program, General Mining, linked with the Oppenheimer Anglo-American Corporation, negotiated with the new regime a deal for bulk-handling of chrome loading equipment.[31]

The same pattern followed in the other decolonized states. In Zambia, when Kaunda grabbed 51-percent share in the Anglo-American owned copper industry, Oppenheimer regarded "government participation" as a welcome move.[32]

[119]

The AAI was never some Marxist lobby, or a group of naïve, wealthy liberals who were tricked into funding Communists. Since its foundation, it acted as a nexus between the U.S. Government and Big Business in shaping post-colonial Africa and providing the personnel for the bureaucracies. The present Chair of the AAI board, Kofi Appenteng, has been employed by Thacher Proffitt & Wood, a corporate law firm; he

---

[30] Africa-America Institute, "Past Programs," accessed May 1, 2012, http://www.aaionline.org/programs/past-programs/southern-african-refugee-education-project-sarep-1976-%E2%80%93-1981/.

[31] Ivor Benson, *The Struggle for Africa* (Perth: Australian League of Rights, 1978), 54.

[32] *Ibid.*, 47.

is a lifetime member of the Council on Foreign Relations and is on the board of the Ford Foundation.[33] The President and CEO of AAI is Mora McLean, who came from the Ford Foundation and is a CFR member.[34]

It would be naïve to think that the United States, in conjunction with the global financial powers, have trained

[33] The reader should not be confused into thinking that because the Ford family does not run the Ford Foundation, that it is a body that has been infiltrated and controlled by Leftists, rather than functioning in the service of plutocracy. Ford and other such Foundations are run by directors and trustees affiliated with Big Business. (See also Bolton, *Revolution from Above*.)

[34] Members of the Board include: William Asiko, President of The Coca-Cola Africa Foundation & Director of Public Affairs and Communications for The Coca-Cola Company in Africa; Rosalind Kainyah, ex-Director of Public Affairs, USA for the De Beers Group, the Oppenheimer mining conglomerate; George Kirkland, Executive Vice President, Chevron Corporation; Carlton Masters, President & CEO, GoodWorks International, a CFR member; Steven Pfeiffer, Chair, Executive Committee, Fulbright & Jaworski LLP, corporate law firm, a CFR member; Maurice Tempelsman, past Chairman AAI; Senior Partner, Leon Tempelsman & Son, (involved with mining, investments and business development), and "Chairman of the Board of Directors of Lazare Kaplan International Inc., the largest cutter and polisher of 'ideal cut' diamonds in the United States"; member of the International Advisory Council of the American Stock Exchange; member of the CFR, etc. AAI, 'Board', accessed May 1, 2012, http://www.aaionline.org/about-aai/board/.

The AAI provides a few profiles of the 23,000 they have trained, such as: Joy Phumaphi, Botswana, Vice President and Head of the World Bank Human Development Network; Dr Mbuyamu I Matungulu, Congo, Mission Chief to Benin, International Monetary Fund; Charles Boamah, Controller and Director, African Development Bank; H E Nahas Angula, Prime Minister, Republic of Namibia; Mamadou Dia (Senegal) Country Director for Cote d'Ivoire and Guinea, Africa Region, World Bank; Dr Renosi Mokate, Deputy Governor, South African Reserve Bank, et al. AAI, 'Alumni Profiles', accessed May 1, 2012 http://www.aaionline.org/alumni-network/alumni-profiles/.

23,000 Africans to take over post-colonial Africa simply as a humanitarian gesture. As of 2008, some of the sponsors of AAI include: Barrick Gold Corporation, Citibank, Coca-Cola Africa, Coca-Cola Africa Foundation, Credit Suisse, Chevron, De Beers Group, Exxon Mobil Corporation, Fulbright and Jaworski LLP, Global Alumina, Goldman Sachs & Co., H J Heinz Co., J P Morgan Chase, Lazare Kaplan International Inc., PepsiCo, Inc., Shell International Limited, Thacher Proffitt & Wood LLP, American Express Foundation, International Finance Corporation, *et al.*[35] AAI is honeycombed with CFR members, as well as luminaries of the Money Power such as Goldman Sachs, Oppenheimer, and Rockefeller interests.

What should not be lost in this analysis is that international [121] power politics and Cold War rivalries were being played out over the corpses of the White settlers. Holden Roberto, the West's "moderate" alternative to Soviet-backed leaders, was later to recall that when his gang invaded from their base in the Congo in 1961, over-running farms, government outposts, and trading centers, "this time the slaves did not cower. They massacred everything."[36] The "liberated" Black-run state of Mozambique inaugurated a 27-year civil war between Roberto's FNLA and the Soviet-backed People's Movement for the Liberation of Angola (MPLA), which accounted for 500,000 deaths.

---

[35]   AAI, "Supporters," accessed May 1, 2012, http://www.aaionline.org/support-aai/supporters/.

[36]   "Holden Roberto dies at 84, Fought to Free Angola from Portuguese Rule," *New York Times*, August 4, 2007.

RHODESIA AND SOUTH AFRICA

The destruction of White rule in the Portuguese Territories was the beginning of the end for the White geopolitical bloc of Southern Africa. Rhodesia was targeted next. In 1965, R.D. McClelland, U.S. Consul-General in Rhodesia, gave the American green light to the terrorists when he stated,

> *[T]here is as much legitimacy in revolution as there is in government. To be other than a revolutionary is to defend the status quo, and the status quo was colonialism. It is the innate role of the revolutionary, and this applies a fortiori to the still white-dominated southern part of the Continent, to change an existing and unsatisfactory order.*[37]

[122]

Pressure began to be applied on Rhodesia when Henry Kissinger met with South Africa's Vorster to lay down the law on the northern neighbor, while simultaneously "South Africa suddenly found the money taps of America and Europe inexplicably turned off," according to G. Sutton, editor of the *South African Financial Mail.*

The strategy to destroy White rule in Rhodesia followed a familiar tactic: a pincer movement of terrorism from below and economic pressure from above. These names stand out in the elimination of White rule:

---

[37]   Quoted by Benson, *This Worldwide Conspiracy*, 69.

- Lord Soames, last Governor of Rhodesia, installed for the purpose of handing over political power, was a director of N. M. Rothschild & Sons and the National Westminster Bank;

- "Tiny" Rowland, CEO of Lonhro, involved in brokering the Lancaster House talks of 1979, which settled the political future of Rhodesia;

- British Foreign Minister Lord Carrington, a director of Hambros Bank, Chairman of ANZ Bank, and a member of the Rockefeller globalist think-tank The Trilateral Commission; chairman of the globalist Bilderberg Group, and a member of Kissinger Associates, the global consultancy firm of omnipresent former U.S. Secretary of State Henry Kissinger.

[123]

South Africa, the final redoubt of White rule anywhere in the world, lost its vision after the assassination of Prime Minister Hendrik Verwoerd in 1966.[38] And much like the Portuguese Salazar and Marcelo Caetano, Verwoerd knew precisely what the forces were at work against White authority, saying of Harry Oppenheimer's economic empire: "With all that money power and with his powerful machine which is spread over the whole country, he can, if he so chooses, exercise enormous interference against the Government and against the state."[39]

---

[38] K.R. Bolton, "Apartheid: Lest We Forget (Or Never Knew)," *Counter-Currents*, accessed May 1, 2012, http://www.counter-currents.com/2011/09/Apartheid-lest-we-forget-or-never-knew/.

[39] David Pallister, Sarah Stewart, and Ian Lepper, *South Africa Inc.: The Oppenheimer Empire* (London: Corgi Books, 1988), 98.

Oppenheimer, for his part, stated flatly why the Money Power opposed White authority in Africa—and it has nothing to do with any humanitarian ideals: "Nationalist politics have made it impossible to make use of Black labour."[40]

LEGACY

Way back in 1959, J.G. van der Meersch of the international banks J.H. Whitney and Dillon Reed & Co. formed the American-Eurafrican Development Corporation, "with the object of meeting the financial needs of emerging African nations when the former colonial powers left."[41] Mr. van der Meersch explained what lay behind the façade of "human rights," "equality," "decolonization," "opposition to Apartheid," and the other facile slogans that were used to remove White rule from Africa and replace it with cosmopolitan finance.

[124]

In 1996, Mandela affirmed that "privatisation is the fundamental policy of the ANC and will remain so"[42]; he set about selling off the state-owned corporations, the *parastatals*, as a legacy of Apartheid. Saint Mandela's "long road to freedom" dismantled the Boer's nationalist economy and replaced it with one much more pleasing to the Lords of High Finance.

---

[40]   *Ibid.*, 80.

[41]   Cited by A.K. Chesterton, *Candour*, July 22, 1960.

[42]   Nelson Mandela, *Financial Mail*, June 7, 1996.

In human terms, since "liberation" in 1994, over 3,000 White farmers have been killed.[43] The old ANC slogan is again popular: "One settler, one bullet!" "Kill the Boer, kill the farmer!" *"Maak dood die wit man"* ("Kill the white man").

In former Rhodesia, 4,000 farmers have been driven from their land. It would, however, be an error to think that the Blacks are the sole benefactors of the land policy. The biggest landowner in Zimbabwe is a Jewish plutocrat. Nicholas Hoogstraten, along with the late "Tiny" Rowland of Lohnro Corp. (mentioned previously), were the main patrons of rival terrorist leaders Robert Mugabe and Joshua Nkomo, respectively. Hoogstraten first purchased land in Rhodesia in 1963, and after he met Rowland, the pair agreed to each back one of the two main Black terrorist leaders. (Hoogstraten, "like any canny businessman, did a bit of betting on both sides."[44]

[125]

Hoogstraten views Zimbabwe farmers as mere "white trash"[45] and made no protest as the government confiscated their property and doled it out to favored Blacks. In 2006, Hoogstraten had a British TV crew from Channel 4 put under

[43]   D. McDougall, "White Farmers 'Being wiped Out,'" *Times* (London), 28 March, 2010, reproduced on *American Renaissance*, accessed May 1, 2012, http://www.amren.com/mtnews/archives/2010/03/white_farmers_b.php.

[44]   David Black, "An Aristocrat of Africa," *Daily Mail & Guardian*, November 26, 1999.

[45]   Basildon Peta, "Van Hoogstraten to take over top bank and colliery in Zimbabwe," 14 July, 2005, DemocraticUnderground.com, accessed May 1, 2012, http://www.democraticunderground.com/discuss/duboard.php?az=view_all&address=102x1627138.

house arrest when he learnt they were to make a documentary critical of Mugabe, and retorted that "if they stepped out of line, I would deal with them personally."[46] A 2006 report stated that he had become "Mugabe's most prominent friend in international business," after John Bredenkamp fled, having backed a losing faction in Mugabe Zimbabwe African National Union-Patriotic Front. "Mr. van Hoogstraten, who has a vast ranch in central Zimbabwe which has not been seized by the president's supporters, has spoken frequently of his friendship with Mr. Mugabe, and said recently that he had lent him $10m, although Mr. Mugabe's spokesman later denied it."[47]

In 2005, Hoogstraten, following the same pattern as Big Money in other African "socialist" states, became "the majority shareholder in Zimbabwe's leading coal producing company...and has a controlling stake in the National Merchant Bank."[48] He is now the second biggest shareholder in Hwange Colliery Company Limited, and has numerous other important investments.[49]

---

[46] He might not have been bluffing. In 2002, Hoogstraten was sentenced to 10 years in prison for the alleged contract killing of a business rival. This verdict was later overturned on appeal; however, after losing a civil case, Hoogstraten was ordered to pay the victim's family £6 million.

[47] A. Meldrum, "Tycoon Flees Zimbabwe After Falling Foul of Mugabe," *The Guardian*, June 9, 2006, accessed May 1, 2012, http://www. guardian.co.uk/world/2006/jun/09/zimbabwe.topstories3.

[48] Peta, *op. cit.*

[49] D. Ndlela, "Hwange Crisis—Gratifying Van Hoogstraten's Rancour," AllAfrica.com, August 17, 2011, accessed May 1, 2012, http://allafrica.com/stories/201108191237.html.

§

While conservatives feared the encroaching spectre of Communism and the USSR throughout the Dark Continent, and hence the capture of the mineral resources and strategic positions, in retrospect, they were blind-sided. The "Soviet menace" allowed the Money Power to establish its hegemony over Africa on the pretext of "stopping Communism," and in so doing eliminated the White settlers, often with bloody consequences that have not yet concluded. ⁊☚

[127]

The

LONG GOODBYE

EDMUND CONNELLY

For a century,
Hollywood
entertained
White Americans
with depictions
of their
dispossession.

EDMUND CONNELLY
is the *nom de plume* of an academic
film and television scholar. He is
a frequent contributor to
The Occidental Quarterly and
The Occidental Observer.

[*images*]
"Hollywoodland"
Advertisement for original Hollywood
housing development, circa 1923.
Wikimedia

"Fat, White, & Dumb"
Ethan Suplee
Shutterstock

In the 1999 detective film *8mm,* [131] Nicolas Cage appears as private investigator Tom Welles. He has been summoned by one Mrs. Christian, a wealthy old widow, to determine the provenance of a pornographic 8mm film found in her late husband's safe. An attorney for the family explains that it appears to be a "snuff film," depicting the sadistic murder of a young woman for sexual-gratification purposes. The film, he believes, is a cheap imitation done with special effects and is therefore nothing to worry about. The widow, however, wants definitive proof and asks Mr. Welles to investigate. The conclusion, sadly, is that the murder is real, having been commissioned by the late Mr. Christian himself. Upon hearing the news, Mrs. Christian takes her own life, leaving for the detective a note reading "Try to forget us."

8mm deserves attention, for it can be read as graphically illustrating a larger agenda aimed at deconstructing the edifices of White European civilization. The museum of European history—the culture, art, and architecture—is depicted as a mask on dark, unspeakable violence and oppression. "Christians," like the widow in *8mm*, are either hypocritical or self-deluding. If they gaze honestly on their past and their identity, they fall into paralysis and despondency. They ultimately seek to erase any memory of their ever having existed, or commit suicide as a means of expatiating their civilizational and racial guilt.

Hollywood films—and their close cousins, TV shows—are appropriate cultural artifacts to parse in an attempt to understand the ongoing effort to displace Majority Americans. While the effort parallels those occurring in other areas of life, such as higher education, government programs, and the legal system, film predates the onset of aggressive anti-White behavior in the latter fields and gives a clearer narrative of what the displacement script looks like. Most crucially, perhaps, is the fact that Hollywood is an empire that from the beginning has been ruled by a hostile elite that has spearheaded White erasure.

The relationship between elites in the United States and (increasingly global) mass culture is complicated and defined by a variety of factors and forces. In this essay, I focus on the *Jewish* elite within the entertainment industry, as well as the peculiarly Jewish character to many Hollywood productions.[1] Jews have held a dominant role in the west-coast film industry

[1]   See Neil Gabler, *An Empire of Their Own: How the Jews Invented Hollywood* (New York: Crown, 1998).

for at least a century; the history of Hollywood thus offers a broad demonstration of how this elite sought to entertain the American Majority, while instilling in Whites the value that true progress is made when they are displaced from positions of power and influence.[2]

Since White Europeans constituted the vast majority of Americans until the 1965 Immigration Act noticeably began to alter the racial composition of the country, Hollywood in the past had to avoid offending or alarming the Majority, who were, after all, the primary consumers of Hollywood fare. As Jews were active both in-front and behind camera, "crypsis" was, in Hollywood's early days, quite widespread. This was a process by which members of the Hollywood inner party "passed" as European Americans. The most elemental step was to adopt a name that mimicked typical Christian surnames.

[133]

---

[2] The question of *why* Jews comprise a hostile elite is complicated, but it has been ably discussed in the voluminous writings of Kevin MacDonald, who identified one Jewish motive as the wish to combat anti-Semitism. (See especially *Separation and Its Discontents: Toward an Evolutionary Theory of Anti-Semitism* (Westport, CT: Praeger, 1998), chapter 6.) The gist of his argument, made over the last 15 years, is that film is perceived by Jews as a method of social engineering and control, which, because they are acutely preoccupied with anti-Semitism, they use, with various degrees of consciousness or unconsciousness, to make White Majority societies in the West safe for Jews. This involves neutralizing Whites by reducing their sense of racial identification and community and increasing racial diversity in their societies. This process may involve different things in the minds of individual Jews, and may result in different outcomes, which may, in turn, be consciously or unconsciously pursued—or not. What the process always implies, however, is the perception of Whites as a resource and/or an obstacle: a resource in as much as they can be exploited as consumers of a passive mind-shaping activity and an obstacle in as much as they may be resistant to deracination or harbor persistent subterranean anti-Semitism.

Also important and revealing were the ways in which Hollywood would depict minority elements in the American nation. The most conspicuous non-White group was, of course, the 12 percent of Americans derived from African ancestry. Hollywood—against most sentiments of the day—began to cast Blacks in roles that both challenged Majority hegemony and created a false image of Black accomplishment and benignity. One can see this clearly when viewing the arc of Hollywood casting over 100 years. As I wrote elsewhere:

[134]

> *Blacks in early American films were portrayed in an overwhelmingly negative light. At best, they were faithful servants and childlike buffoons. At worst, they were irresponsible, impulsive, lustful, and violent. One of the first major motion picture features ever made was D. W. Griffith's* Birth of a Nation *(1915), based on Thomas W. Dixon's novel and stage melodrama* The Clansman, *which portrayed recently emancipated slaves rising up against the white order, raping white women, and visiting violence upon white Americans in general. Since* Birth of a Nation, *the celluloid images of both blacks and whites in America have undergone an almost perfect reversal.*[3]

Consider the 1958 film *The Vikings*, starring Ernest Borgnine, Kirk Douglas, and Tony Curtis, and directed by

---

[3] Edmund Connelly, "Understanding Hollywood," Part III: "Racial Role-Reversals," *The Occidental Quarterly*, vol. 9, no. 2 (Summer 2009).

Richard Fleischer. While in some senses a case of crypsis (Douglas and Curtis were both Jewish and had changed their surnames), it is more properly seen as an early instance of gradual White replacement; the Norse saga had two Jews acting as Vikings, and the non-Jewish but still ethnic Borgnine (né Borgnino) as a powerful Viking king. Director Fleischer was also Jewish, the son of Essie (née Goldstein) and animator/producer Max Fleischer, so one can assume they were quite aware of the ethnic dimension to the film's casting. (Incidentally, a logical conclusion to this process is the casting of Black actor Idris Elba as a Nordic god in the 2011 film *Thor*).

Beyond ethnic reshuffling, Hollywood used a host of other subtle techniques to recast the American nation. A stand-out example was *All in the Family* (1971-1975), the hugely popular sitcom created by Norman Lear. There, Archie Bunker, the head of the family, was presented as a crude but likable bigot, who underwent changes of heart as the series progressed. Moreover, he taught his audience how ridiculous efforts of White men like himself to preserve their culture and country were. The ultimate propaganda of Archie Bunker is that after cracking wise in a racialist manner, he would eventually return to his easy chair and sit passively as the world was transformed around him.

[135]

Just after the Second World War, a sophisticated campaign was launched in America to launder out what mild anti-Semitism might still exist. First came, in 1947, the novel *Gentleman's Agreement*, written by Laura Z. Hobson, daughter of editor of *The Jewish Daily Forward*, Michael Zametkin. Thereafter, this bestselling novel became a Hollywood box-office hit in a film of the same name. Starring Gregory Peck as a Gentile reporter investigating the purported scourge of social anti-Semitism, the film joined the novel in lecturing that anti-Jewish animus in any form was not to be accepted by decent Americans. The novel appeared in April of that year, followed by a full-blown film only months later. (The pair were clearly planned in advanced as a two-pronged effort.) The resulting critique attacked the Majority's desire to maintain borders around its institutions and cultural prerogatives, actions which are, really, no more than normal defensive measures seen in every healthy culture.

[136]

      The 1960s, however, witnessed a great awakening of *open* Jewish sensibilities, and screen fare reflected this shift, as film scholar Patricia Erens attests:

> *With the arrival of the 1960s, the representation of the Jew on the American screen bursts into full bloom. Not since the 1920s have so many Jewish characters appeared, especially in major roles. Once again the Jewish family emerges as a central theme. Likewise, Jewish domestic comedy makes a reappearance, and the majority of Jewish characters are played by Jewish actors and actresses . . . In short, the late 1960s and 1970s become a second Golden Age for Jews on the screen.*[4]

------

[4]   Patricia Erens, *The Jew in American Cinema* (Bloomington: Indiana University Press, 1984), 257.

American cultural historian Stephen Whitfield concurs with this assessment. Following the wild success of the 1960 film adaptation of Leon Uris's novel *Exodus* (which chronicled the birth of modern Israel) came, according to Whitfield,

> *an almost exultant revelation in the fortuitous fact of Jewishness, with sprinklings of minor characters and occasional phrases soon overwhelmed by whole movies devoted to the residual mysteries of modern Jewish identity. The stars, for example, began to preserve their names. . . . Jeff Goldblum kept his name; and a gentile, Caryn Johnson, actually changed hers to Whoopi Goldberg. . . . the Indians not only bore odd resemblances to Hollywood Jews, but even began speaking Yiddish, as in Elliot Silverstein's* Cat Ballou *(1965).*

[137]

> *When a black cabbie (in* Bye Bye Braverman*) and a Japanese career woman (in* Walk, Don't Run*) speak Yiddish, when Jewishness is introduced no matter how irrelevant the context, even moviegoers deprived of seeing Jewish roles for three decades earlier might have echoed the sentiment of the passenger who was standing at the liquor bar of the Titanic, just as the liner collided with fate: "I did ask for ice, but this is too much."*[5]

The 1967 film *The Graduate*, featuring Dustin Hoffman as Ben Braddock, nicely encapsulates the rise of

---

[5]   Stephen J. Whitfield, *American Space, Jewish Time: Essays in Modern Culture and Politics* (Armonk, NY: M.E. Sharpe, Inc., 1996), 164-166.

Jewish sensibilities in American cinema. The movie uses WASP characters and settings throughout, but these serve mainly to mask certain Jewish undercurrents, including a hostility towards elite Gentile culture. The film's climatic scene reveals these energies in an almost grotesque fashion. Here, Hoffman's Braddock races to the church to break up his true love's marriage to a blond Christian. In a scene powerful for its symbolism, Ben arrives at the church too late; his love has just pronounced her "I do" and is kissing her new husband. Climbing into the second-floor choir loft, Ben screams out her name: *"Elaine! Elaine!"* Turning to him, Elaine realizes that Ben is the better choice, and she abandons both altar and new husband to be with him.

[138] Before getting away, however, Ben faces a bevy of furious Gentiles, including Elaine's father, Mr. Robinson, whom Ben has earlier cuckolded. Grappling at the foot of the church stairs, Ben delivers a blow to the gut, and Mr. Robinson falls. Next, Ben faces the swarm of blond-haired young men, sparkling white teeth flashing in the crystal light of the church. To defeat them, he grabs a gilded five-foot cross and swings it wildly into the seething flock of Christians. Keeping them momentarily at bay, he takes Elaine outside the church and bars the doors with the cross, completing his escape.

The Graduate was directed by Mike Nichols, "an immigrant from Danzig, who had stepped off the Bremen right before World War II"[6] Nichols found that "the deeper he got

---

[6]   Whitfield, 60.

into the shoot and the more intensely he pushed Hoffman past what the actor thought he could withstand, the more Nichols realized that something painful and personal was at stake, and always had been, in his attraction to the story."

> *"My unconscious was making this movie," he says. "It took me years before I got what I had been doing all along—that I had been turning Benjamin into a Jew. I didn't get it until I saw this hilarious issue of* MAD *magazine after the movie came out, in which the caricature of Dustin says to the caricature of Elizabeth Wilson, "Mom, how come I'm Jewish and you and Dad aren't?" And I asked myself the same question, and the answer was fairly embarrassing and fairly obvious."*[7]

[139]

Appreciating Braddock's cryptic identity, his love affairs with both Elaine and her mother ("Mrs. Robinson") takes on a new meaning: Braddock succeeds in besting elite WASP society as well as conquering two *shikses*.

The Graduate appeared in the same year as Philip Roth's novel *Portnoy's Complaint*, and the parallel sentiments toward the *shiksa* are revealing. As the titular character explains: "*Shikses*! In winter, when the polio germs are hibernating and I can bank upon surviving outside of an iron lung until the end of

---

[7]   Mark Harris, "Book Excerpt: Inside the Making of 'The Graduate,'" *Entertainment Weekly*, Feburary 10, 2008, accessed September 1, 2012, http://www.ew.com/ew/article/0,,20176758,00.html.

the school year, I ice-skate on the lake in Irvington Park. . . . I skate round and round in circles behind the *shikses* who live in Irvington. . . But the *shikses*, ah, the *shikses* are something else again."

While lusting after young blonde Gentile women, however, the greater theme is one of hostility toward the broader WASP culture. Roth made this clear, too, when he mocked the rise and fall of Columbia University instructor Charles Van Doren, a highly decorated intellectual who confessed to having cheated on the nationally televised quiz show *Twenty One*. Roth inserts a scene into *Portnoy's Complaint*:

> *I was on the staff of the House subcommittee investigating the television scandals. . . . and then of course that extra bonus, Charlatan Van Doren. Such character, such brains and breeding . . . And turns out he's a fake. Well, what do you know about that, Gentile America? Supergoy, a gonif! Steals money. Covets money. Wants money, will do anything for it. Goodness gracious me, almost as bad as Jews—you sanctimonious WASPs!*
>
> *Yes, I was one happy yiddel down there in Washington, a little Stern gang of my own, busily exploding Charlie's honor and integrity, while simultaneously becoming lover to that aristocratic Yankee beauty whose forebears arrived on these shores in the seventeenth century. Phenomenon known as Hating Your Goy and Eating One Too.*[8]

---

[8]   Roth, *Portnoy's Complaint*, 232-233. Roth mined this incident more thoroughly in his 1981 novel, *Zuckerman Unbound* (New York), 33-40.

The dominance of European-derived people in the United States soon took further blows in popular culture. Many Baby Boomers grew up on the classic sitcoms of the era, *Gilligan's Island, I Dream of Jeannie, The Brady Bunch etc.* Though created by Jewish writers and producers, these programs amounted mostly to harmless fun. Even the "hayseed" shows about the heartland and American Majority had all-White casts and generally treated their characters with respect. By the early 1970s, however, all these had vanished from the three major networks' evening offerings and were replaced by decidedly more ethnic fare. Gone were *The Beverly Hillbillies, The Andy Griffith Show/Mayberry R.F.D., Green Acres,* and *Petticoat Junction.* In their stead came "hip, urban" shows that "pushed the socially engaged agenda into the ethno-racial arena." Out with Andy Griffith and Don Knotts and in with "ethnicoms" like *Sanford and Son, The Jeffersons,* and *Chico and the Man.*[9] Further, these socially conscious sitcoms were often critical of mainstream values, led, as mentioned above, by Norman Lear's *All in the Family.*

[141]

The culmination of this trend was not *Sanford and Son* but *The Cosby Show*—that is, not shows featuring down-and-out, if likable Negroes but ones that depicted Blacks as morally and intellectually superior. Richard Brookhiser memorably termed this reverence for the "Numinous Negro."[10]

---

[9] Vincent Brook, *Something Ain't Kosher Here: The Rise of the "Jewish" Sitcom* (New Brunswick, New Jersey: Rutgers University Press, 2003), 49.

[10] Richard Brookhiser, "The Numinous Negro—His importance in our lives; why he is fading," *National Review,* August 20, 2001.

The most obvious example comes in the person of Morgan Freeman in films such as *The Shawshank Redemption* (1994), *Deep Impact* (1998; in which he depicts a U.S. president), and *Bruce Almighty* (2003; where he plays none other than God). Consider that by 1998, when Freeman played the role of a kindly Commander-in-Chief in *Deep Impact*, his persona was fixed as the intelligent moral center of each of his films. Steve Sailer aptly dubbed Freeman America's "Spiritual Presence-in-Chief." He also noted how millions of Americans "want Will Smith to be their Hero-in-Chief. . . . Some want James Earl Jones, the Lion King himself, to be their Father-in-Chief."[11]

Denzel Washington has long been a younger version of the Numinous Negro, having starred in a string of high-profile roles as moral and physical heroes. In 1987's *Cry Freedom*, for example, he played South African anti-Apartheid martyr Steve Biko. In 1989's *Glory*, he played an escaped slave who joins the Union army in the Civil War. Washington's big breakthrough, however, was his title role in the 1992 Spike Lee film *Malcolm X*. He later played the lead in *The Hurricane* (1999), about boxer Rubin "Hurricane" Carter, unjustly imprisoned for the 1966 murders of three New Jersey Whites. Other race-charged Washington films include *The Siege* (1998; non-Whites and women are highly empowered), *Antwone Fisher* (2002; a Black seaman deals with the ghosts of White racism), *Déjà Vu* (2006; a White terrorist kills hundreds, including a young black woman;

---

[11] See Steve Sailer, VDARE.com, March 30, 2008, accessed September 1, 2012, http://www.vdare.com/Sailer/080330_obama.htm.

Washington's character tracks him down), *The Great Debaters* (2007; memories of lynchings in the South), *The Book of Eli* (though blind, Washington's character is omnipotent), and *Unstoppable* (both 2010). Regarding the theme of the rise of the Black man at the expense of the White man, however, two of Washington's films stand out: *Crimson Tide* (1995) and *Remember the Titans* (2000), both produced by Jerry Bruckheimer.

I have long argued that the anti-White structure in Hollywood has demanded the creation of model Black men to "teach" the population that such characters are the norm in our new multicultural society. Washington is a well-paid pawn in that project. Both *Crimson Tide* and *Remember the Titans* are allegories for America as a whole; in the first instance, society is represented by the crew of a ballistic missile submarine and in the second, by a newly integrated high-school football team. In both, Washington's characters are upright, moral, and intelligent men, and thus worthy of replacing the White men who have power in the beginning but lose it to the Black man over the course of the narrative.

[143]

As an aside, it is worth noting how Washington's positive characters are contrasted with those of Ethan Suplee, an actor routinely used to portray stupid, fat White men. In the powerful 1998 neo-Nazi film *American History X*, for instance, Suplee was cast not only as a fat White imbecile but as a fat, White skinhead and neo-Nazi imbecile with tattoos and unquenchable hatreds.

Two years later, he began his appearances with Denzel Washington, starting with *Remember the Titans*. Directed by Boaz Yakin and produced by Jerry Bruckheimer, this film is a straightforward replacement film. The script repeatedly shows Suplee as an overtly stupid lineman and always contrasts him with brilliant Blacks. For instance, when they go to football camp in Gettysburg, Pennsylvania (yes, this is used to ruminate on the racism surrounding the Civil War; and yes, they went to camp in a school bus, which is used to educate the audience on the necessity of 1970s desegregation busing ordinances), Suplee is asked by Washington's coach character about his future plans. College? No, the lineman answers, "I'm no brainiac like the Rev," a reference to a Black player. The Black coach then generously offers to tutor the doofus. Later, there is even a scene where the lineman himself blurts out that he's "nothing but no-good White trash." Fortunately, "Rev" Harris is not only smart but kind, and he, too, promises to tutor the hopelessly stupid White man.[12]

Two years later, Suplee again appeared with Washington, this time in a minor role as a stupid security guard at a hospital in the tear-jerker *John Q*. In the film, Blacks are the victims of a heartless healthcare system. In *Unstoppable*, Suplee gets his third appearance with Washington, and, true to form, he is his usual

[12] On television, from 2005-2009, Suplee played Randall "Randy" Dew Hickey, younger brother to Earl on the hit TV series *My Name is Earl*. Wikipedia says that Randy "is thought to be very dimwitted and simple, bordering on mild mental retardation" (Wikipedia, *My Name Is Earl*, accessed September 1, 2012, http://en.wikipedia.org/wiki/My_name_is_earl.

moronic, fat self, in contrast to Washington's tall and muscular figure and scripted brain power. Early in the film, we see Suplee as the dim-witted, lazy engineer "Dewey." Assigned to move a freight train in the yard, he hobbles aboard and gets it moving. When he notices that a switch ahead is out of position, he sets the safety brake and prepares to get out and move the switch himself. Once out of the cab, the engine kicks into full throttle on its own accord, and Dewey is faced with the task of chasing it down, re-boarding, and taking back control of the empty train. Because he is so fat and out of shape, he can barely keep up with the slow-moving train and falls face first into the stone ballast alongside the train. Now they have a "coaster" on their hands.

This allows for a pronounced propaganda message [145] when Puerto Rican yardmaster Connie Hooper (Rosario Dawson) berates Dewey and his partner when the train "gets away" from them. "It's a train, Dewey, not a chipmunk." The knock-out message, however, comes with this sassy New York City girl's confrontation with her supervisor, Oscar Galvin, an overweight, overbearing White man. Repeatedly, his plans to stop the train fail and nearly lead to disaster, while Hooper's plans would have worked. In the end, Washington's elder wise character, in conjunction with a wet-behind-the-collar rookie White man, save the train, and multicultural America lives happily ever after.

Such portrayals have consequences. Consider, for example, how an unaccomplished Black man ever became

President of the United States. One suspects that without prior preparing of the mind, tens of millions of White Americans may have balked at electing Barack Obama. The preparation came not only in film but in television as well, the prime source being the government anti-terrorist action drama *24*. Season One began with a Black presidential candidate, David Palmer. The *Los Angeles Times*'s Hollywood beat reporter, Joel Stein, shows the impact of this show on Obama's successful run for president:

> *Hollywood has warmed us up already, namely with Morgan Freeman in* Deep Impact *and Dennis Haysbert in 24. . . . Obama is strikingly similar to Haysbert's character, President David Palmer: Both were senators, both campaigned in their mid-40s and both deliver JFK-style speeches in a cool, jazz baritone. "I think we both have a similar approach to who and what we believe the president is. Barack doesn't get angry. He's pretty level. That's how I portrayed President Palmer: as a man with control over his emotions and great intelligence," Haysbert says.* [13]

In an *Atlantic Monthly* cover story, Vassar professor Hua Hsu details the progressive denigration of the White man's image on television:

> *Successful network-television shows like* Lost, Heroes, *and* Grey's Anatomy *feature wildly diverse casts, and an entire genre of half-hour comedy,*

---

[13] Joel Stein, "A Black President? Seen a Few," *Los Angeles Times*, January 11, 2008.

from The Colbert Report *to* The Office, *seems dedicated to having fun with the persona of the clueless white male. The youth market is following the same pattern. . . .*

Pop culture today rallies around an ethic of multicultural inclusion that seems to value every identity—except whiteness. "It's becoming harder for the blond-haired, blue-eyed commercial actor."[14]

Such observations appear common. Ironically, a writer for the Jewish magazine *Commentary* recently wrote that a current "spate of books and essays about the decline of men notes that in measures of educational achievement, women are outperforming men, and in the workplace they are poised to dominate in the fields that are the most likely to succeed in the new global economy." Sure enough, "Popular culture serves up images of slacker men tethered to their video-game consoles and bumbling fathers dominated by hyper-efficient *über*-women who regularly berate them for their incompetence, adding to the overall picture of male failure." The question necessarily asked is "Why are they behind in measures of educational achievement? Why have they borne the brunt of the recent economic downturn? What does this mean for the future of manhood?" [15] Precisely.

[147]

---

[14] Hua Hsu, "The End of White America?" *The Atlantic Monthly,* January/February 2009; Quoted in Patrick J. Buchanan, *Suicide of a Superpower: Will America Survive to 2025?* (New York: Thomas Dunne Books, 2011), 125-126.

[15] Christine Rosen, "Vive la Différence Feminism," *Commentary,* January 2012, 44.

Richard Spencer, editor of this new journal, has described the White man as "liv[ing] in a world his race once dominated—and in which Black and Brown are now colonizers, in which European heritage is being taken away piece by piece: cultural heroes, literature, popular icons, identity—ultimately, everything." The lingering question is how much longer White men will remain passive viewers of these false images. Needless to say, should it continue much longer, Hollywood's scripted erasure of Whiteness will meld with the actual disappearance of the White race. ⁊

[148]

The

DISPOSSESSED ELITE

KEVIN MACDONALD

*In the multiracial,
postmodern world,
the Anglo-Saxon
Protestant has become
the identity that dare
not speak its name.
Kevin MacDonald
goes in search of the
forbidden race.*

KEVIN MACDONALD
is Professor of Psychology at
California State University–
Long Beach. He is the author
of more than 100 scholarly
papers and reviews, as well
as *A People That Shall Dwell
Alone: Judaism as a Group
Evolutionary Strategy* (1994),
*Separation and Its Discontents:
Toward an Evolutionary Theory
of Anti-Semitism* (1998),
and *The Culture of Critique:
An Evolutionary Analysis
of Jewish Involvement in
Twentieth-Century Intellectual
and Political Movements*
(1998). He is Editor of *The
Occidental Observer* and *The
Occidental Quarterly*. *Cultural
Insurrections*, a collection of
essays, appeared in 2008.

Andrew Fraser is a

legal scholar who has been forced to brave the slings and arrows of outrageous anti-White attitude in his position as Professor of Public Law at Macquarie University in Sydney. His book *The WASP Question* is a detailed presentation of his views on the self-destruction of the once-proud group of Anglo-Saxons who colonized vast areas after departing from their native England, but who are now very much threatened by loss of power and, even more disastrously, loss of identity. The book is an attempt to answer the question why WASPs (which he describes as "a subtly, perhaps deservedly derogatory acronym coined sometime in the late Fifties to denote White Anglo-Saxon Protestants") have failed to protect their bio-cultural interests in the contemporary world.

This is indeed the fundamental question of our times—true not only of WASPs, but of all Whites, although it must be said that WASPs seem to embody this pathology to a greater extent than other White groups. Fraser's answer is an intellectual *tour de force*, encompassing very wide swaths of history and pre-history, evolutionary thinking, the psychology of racial differences, and academic theology. Far from being a paean to his ethnic group, the book is nothing less than "an *attack* on my co-ethnics, mainly the American WASPs who for over two centuries now have waged a reckless, revolutionary, and relentless cultural war on the ethno-religious traditions which once inspired the Anglo-Saxon province of Christendom to greatness."

[154]

At the heart of this project is an attempt to understand WASP uniqueness. As he notes early on, "European man alone bears the spirit of civic republicanism, a tradition still largely alien to other races and peoples." Whereas WASPs eschew ethnic nepotism as a matter of enlightened principle, "there is no shortage of evidence that the Changs, the Gonzales, and the Singhs (not to mention the Goldmans with their well-known animus toward WASPs) still practice forms of ethnic nepotism strictly forbidden to Anglo-Protestants."

Fraser's search for unraveling this mystery begins with the Germanic origins of Anglo-Saxon society. Relying on recent population genetic data, Fraser suggests that beginning in the mid-5th century, the Angle, Saxon, and Jute invaders contributed beyond their numbers to the gene pool of what was to become England. Males from indigenous Britons were forced to migrate to the outer reaches of the island, but with high levels of intermarriage with native women. The result was that the population was distinct from the Germanic groups left behind on the continent.

Fraser points to "an institutionalized predisposition towards both local autonomy and individual liberty" as characteristic of Northern European peoples, based on monogamy, the nuclear family, paternal investment in children, and a relative de-emphasis on extended kinship groups, leading to the rise of non-kinship-based forms of reciprocity. These traits were adaptive when confronting difficult ecological conditions during the Ice Ages.

[155]

However, these tribal groups also had a strong sense of internal cohesion and in-group solidarity, and kinship ties were, indeed, of considerable importance, as indicated by the long history of blood feud and *wergeld*.

An important manifestation of non-kinship-based reciprocity was the *Männerbund* or *comitatus*—groups formed for military purposes and based on the reputation of leaders and the followers rather than on their kinship relatedness. Indeed, Fraser quotes James Russell (from *The Germanization of Early Medieval Christianity*[1]): "The intensity of the comitatus bond seems to exceed even that of kinship."

---

[1] James Russell, *The Germanization of Early Medieval Christianity: A Sociohistorical Approach to Religious Transformation* (Oxford and New York: Oxford University Press, 1996).

Fraser makes the interesting point that "there were striking differences in the relative importance of lordship and kinship in Anglo-Saxon England,"

> *as compared with southern Denmark and northern Germany from which the Angles, the Jutes and the Saxons originated. In Friesland and Schleswig-Holstein, throughout the Middle Ages there was a preponderance of free peasant proprietors with few great territorial lords endowed with seigneurial privileges. In England, by contrast, the prevalence of lordship was much more marked.*

[156] Based on Berta Surees Phillipotts' wonderfully titled *Kindred and Clan in the Middle Ages and After: A Study in the Sociology of the Teutonic Races*[2], there is the suggestion that these differences were caused by the relative lack of strength of kinship groups in areas, like England, that became dominated by lords. According to this hypothesis, kinship relationships were compromised as Germanic groups left their native areas in southern Sweden, Denmark, and northern Germany.

Anglo-Saxon kings possessed "a sacral quality by virtue of their royal blood." Kings combined religious and political functions, and their relationships with their subjects were ultimately based on reciprocity. And because kingship had religious overtones, "the ethnogenesis of the English people was

---

[2]   Berta Surees Phillipotts, *Kindred and Clan in the Middle Ages and After: A Study in the Sociology of the Teutonic Races* (Cambridge: Cambridge University Press, 1913).

very largely a religious phenomenon, proceeding in tandem with the success of Christian missionaries into the fold of the Church. By the 8th century the *Angelcynn*—people of the English race— had been formed from the mélange of Germanic tribes that had entered England."

This shift to Christianity was accomplished without losing touch with Germanic folk religions. The Norman conquest had no fundamental effect on English institutions, since "Normandy itself had been conquered by sea-borne Teutonic invaders and, as a consequence, kindred groups had been weakened there just as they had been in England. Anglo-Saxon men may have been disinherited by their Norman overlords but 'their daughters married Normans and taught their children the meaning of Englishness,'" quoting Phillpotts.

[157]

Despite the differences among different social groups of Englishmen, there was a common sense of being English based on "common blood nourished by a common faith." Jews were regarded as outsiders precisely because they were not of common blood or common faith, so much so that the *Magna Carta* had clauses explicitly protecting English families from the Jews. Royal responsibility for the welfare of subjects meant that "English kings were compelled eventually to place definite limits on Jewish exploitation of their Christian subjects." Jews were not merely outsiders, but tough economic competitors. When the Church sided with the people by petitioning the king to "protect his people against Jewish economic aggression," the king expelled the Jews, but only after being assured that the revenue they provided to the king would be made up by revenue from the Church and the nobility.

The fact that the king tried first to convert the Jews indicates that European societies were not self-consciously based on blood ties. Attempts to convert Jews were a common phenomenon during the Middle Ages throughout Europe. The only important case where Jews actually converted was in Spain, but then the issue became the sincerity of the converts and their continued ethnic cohesion and cooperation, leading ultimately to the Inquisition.[3] The desire of Europeans to assimilate with the Jews was always a one-way street.

[158]

In the absence of kinship ties, reputation was everything. Fraser spends quite a bit of time on oath-taking as a peculiarly English pre-occupation, so much so that "the commonplace spectacle of Third World immigrants reciting oaths of allegiance at naturalization ceremonies is calculated to warm the hearts of WASPs committed heart and soul to the constitutionalist creed of civic nationalism." Oath-taking is a public affirmation that is fundamentally about one's reputation. It is, of course, a bit of WASP egoism that they think that other peoples have a similar sense of public trustworthiness.

> *WASPs are trusting souls. For that very reason*
> *they can be exploited easily by those who promise*

---

[3]   See K. MacDonald, *Separation and Its Discontents: Toward an Evolutionary Theory of Anti-Semitism* (Westport, CT: Praeger, 1998), Chapters 4 and 7.

one thing and do another. . . . Mass Third World immigration imposes enormous risks upon Anglo-Saxon societies grounded in unique patterns of trusting behavior that evolved over many centuries. If newcomers do not accept the burdens entailed by the civic culture of the host society—most notably the need to forswear one's pre-existing racial, ethnic and religious allegiances—they are bound to reduce the benefits of good citizenship for the host Anglo-Saxon nation.

I couldn't agree more. And all the evidence is that these groups will not forswear these allegiances, any more than Jews have forsworn their ethnic and religious allegiances despite centuries of living among Europeans.

[159]

The next great historical step for the *Angelcynn* was the step from a Germanized Christianity to a far more universalist form of Christianity as a result of the expansion of the power of the centralized Church during the 11th-13th centuries. This momentous process began with the papal reforms of Pope Gregory VII that had as their basic aim an increase in ecclesiastical power at the expense of the kings. The result was a *Kirchenstaat*—Church-state—that eventually compromised the Anglo-Saxon Christian cult of sacral kingship. But rather than a unitary society based on sacral kingship, there was a split between the realm of religion, dominated by the Church, and the secular realm, dominated by the kings. This development also weakened the already fragile ties of kinship, as the Church actively campaigned against endogamy by restricting marriage of relatives and developed a concept of marriage in which the individuals to be married, not relatives, had an absolute right to choose marriage partners.[4]

This development facilitated individualism, and especially among the English. Fraser is aware that the roots of Western individualism may be found in Classical Greece. But "by the thirteenth century, the English were already set apart from the rest of Christendom by their pronounced predisposition towards liberty, independence and individualism"—tendencies that, as he notes, are in stark contrast with the Chinese (and all other cultures of which I am aware).

[160]   Kings responded to the ecclesiastical power grab by setting up their own secular institutions of justice independent of the Church courts. Political authority became "disenchanted"— removed from any connection to the sacred; royal authority became "a function of the king's temporal body politic; no longer was his natural body the medium through which an emanation of sacred *Heil* descended directly from the gods."

Basic to the period was the concept of "double majesty" in which both the king and his leading men had power. This concept was based on the *comitatus* concept—what Ricardo Duchesne terms "aristocratic egalitarianism."[5] The king is first

---

[4]   Kevin MacDonald, "The Establishment and Maintenance of Socially Imposed Monogamy in Western Europe," *Politics and the Life Sciences*, vol. 14, 1995.

[5]   Ricardo Duchesne, *The Uniqueness of Western Civilization* (Leiden, the Netherlands: Brill, 2011).

among equals. He had power, but his acts required the approval of the magnates and they could act to restrain him from rashness. As Fraser notes, the baronial class had power within this system, but the arrangement excluded the "vast majority of ordinary folk." One result was that the great barons retained considerable power over local affairs, while the king tended to affairs that affected the kingdom as a whole.

The Tudor revolution eclipsed both the power of the nobility and the power of the Church. But the events unleashed by this upheaval resulted in an even more revolutionary and radical revolution in English political culture: the rise of the Puritans. The Puritan revolution represented a fundamental break in English history, and Fraser is deeply critical:

[161]

> It was the Puritan refusal to recognize the established Church of England as the synergistic unity of society, politics and religion that finally sealed the fate of the ancient regime in England. Puritans rejected the past-oriented, this-worldly folk religion of their Germanic ancestors and embraced instead a future-oriented, salvation history of sin and redemption in which the "Godly" were radically estranged from conventional society. Separating themselves from their "lukewarm" neighbours, Puritans withdrew into select, independent and voluntary communities composed solely of equals. Their virtuous communities of the elect existed in a state of grace that knew no national boundaries.

The result was "a radically new social character" that resulted in the "*embourgeoisement* of English elites." This New Order cut off the possibility of an Anglican commonwealth; it was focused on the accumulation of wealth for its own sake.

The radicalism of the Puritan Revolution was that it completely destroyed the old tripartite Indo-European order based on the classes of sovereignty, the military, and commoners. This revolution was far more radical than the revolution whereby Christianity destroyed the pagan gods of old Europe:

> *Christianity formally proscribed the old religions but it did not uproot the social ideals embodied in the pagan gods. Even after the Papal Revolution, tradition-directed English Christians preserved the Trinitarian cosmology that their Anglo-Saxon ancestors shared with the Celts, the Scandinavians and the Romans.*
>
> *The Puritan spirit of capitalism not only turned that ancient worldview on its head: it also launched Anglo-Saxons into a novus ordo seclorum that brought religion down to earth in an economy enchanted by the cornucopian myths of modernist Mammonism. ... Before we can hope to escape our self-imposed domination, we must understand how the Puritan Revolution flattened the foundational myths of the trifunctional social order characteristic of all Indo-European peoples.*

In short, the Puritan Revolution meant the end of the Indo-European world and its Christian version: the Church ("those who prayed, *oratores*"), the king and aristocracy ("those who fought, *bellatores*"), and the commoners ("those who worked, *laboratores*"). It was thus the quintessential modern revolution, a fundamental break in the history of the West.

The revolution, although begun in England, was slow to reach its completion there, whereas in the United States, "as a consequence of the Civil War, the absolute hegemony of the leveling, acquisitive and utilitarian society pioneered by the Puritan Revolution was firmly entrenched." The Civil War pitted "the Cavaliers of the Old South [who] recalled the highest ideals of European chivalry" against "the soulless materialism of Northern capitalism."

[163]

The Puritans had won, but in Fraser's analysis, their victory heralded the end of a highly adaptive social order in favor of a social order that eventually led to the eclipse of WASPs. The new order was far more egalitarian than the older order. Congregations elected their ministers, and they served at the pleasure of the people they served. Whereas war had been the province of the nobility, Cromwell's New Model Army was based on citizen participation.

It was also profoundly spiritual and created enormous energy. Unfortunately, the spiritual capital of Puritanism "was squandered by their WASP descendants. The saintly secularism of the Puritan has degenerated into the nonchalant nihilism of the postmodernist." "Possessive individualism" and "tasteful consumption" had come to define the highest expression of Anglo-Saxon character and culture. The governments of England and other Anglo-Saxon areas became dominated by financial interests.

When the intellectuals of the new order looked at the English past, they did not see a social order of liberty and reciprocity. Rather,

> they insisted that "Old England had been steeped in slavery" and only after the Whigs had triumphed in the Glorious Revolution did the English begin to enjoy their present freedoms. ... "To bring the government of England back to its first principles is to bring the people back to absolute slavery." In the dark days of the past, "the people had no share in the government; they were merely the villeins, vassals, or bondsmen of their lords, "a sort of cattle bought and sold with the land." Those slavish ancestors had submitted, more or less willingly, to the yoke fastened on their necks by those who prayed and those who fought. Such a servile mentality, it is said, had no rightful claim to a voice in the political community of the modern English commonwealth.

Indeed, White slavery continued to exist in the New World as indentured servants were bought and sold—"a situation not unlike Negro slavery."

This new social order requires endless economic expansion. If that fails to come to pass, there will indeed be a crisis, and it's clear where Fraser's sympathies lie:

> One hopes that such a state of emergency will trigger the need to return to the long-forgotten original principles of the tripartite social order, however "atavistic" such needs may seem to the modern managerial mind. The day may yet come when ineffectual WASPs give way to a new generation of Anglo-Saxon leaders possessed of both the sovereign wisdom to revive the communitarian ethos of the ancient republics and the selfless nobility to defend unto death the bio-cultural interests of their people.

[165]

However, before discussing in detail his proposal for a return to a primeval Indo-European cultural paradigm, Fraser discusses the rise and fall of WASPs in the United States. His basic proposal is that WASPs are a superior group in terms of IQ and other traits necessary for success in the contemporary world. He accepts the idea that different races and ethnic groups are in competition for survival. This race realist perspective, explicitly based on sociobiology, is combined with the idea that WASP talents should be seen as a gift from God and that WASPs require an ethno-theology capable of serving their biological interests in survival and reproduction. Fraser fundamentally disagrees with the idea that the sacred and secular ought to inhabit two separate worlds. Rather, they should be joined by fostering an ethno-religious sense of peoplehood in which the biological imperatives of survival, reproduction and sense of being part of an ethnic group are embedded in religious belief—a rejection of what he sees as the deformity of Christian theology that occurred as a result of the Medieval papal reforms discussed above. Fraser therefore takes Frank Salter to task for developing a theory of ethnic interests based solely on "mature Enlightenment values"—on reason rather than theology.[6]

Fraser does not see the future as a reconquest of lands once controlled by WASPs, but rather as the creation of WASPs as a diaspora people capable of retaining their ethnic and religious ties in a "postmodern archipelago."

[166]   The Jewish Diaspora based on strong ethno-centrism and in-group altruism and ethnic networking thus becomes the implicit model for a WASP future. As he notes, the original Puritans also had many of the traits that define successful groups—the willingness to suppress individual goals for the good of the group by enacting laws that, for example, prohibited excessive profits.

Part Two deals with America as an experiment in WASP culture, and in particular with "the pathogenesis of Anglo-Saxon Anglophobia." For Fraser, the pathogenesis starts with a rejection of the religious basis of Anglo-Saxon peoplehood. The entire concept of America independent of Britain is anathema: The American

---

[6]   Frank Salter, *On Genetic Interests: Family, Ethny, and Humanity in an Age of Mass Migration* (New Brunswick, NJ: Transaction, 2006).

Revolution "suppressed the spirit of ethnoreligious loyalty owed by all British colonists to the blood and faith of Old England."

Freed of the hereditary aristocracy and the religion of England, during the Jacksonian era, "the few remaining conservative influences in religion, politics, and law" were swept aside. The result was an exultant radical individualism in which every individual was to have direct, unmediated access to God. This radical individualism distrusted all manifestations of corporate power, including chartered private corporations, and Fraser agrees, writing that "a perversion of Christian theology permitted the modern business corporation to establish itself as a secular parody of the *ecclesia.*"

[167]

From a bicultural perspective, the most important consequence of the managerial revolution in corporate governance was the recasting of Anglo-American social character into a novel form, one particularly susceptible to Anglo-Saxon Anglophobia.

The corporation eventually metastasized into a monster "incapable of preserving either the class boundaries of the bourgeoisie or the ethnic character of the Anglo-American nation as a whole." In the hands of recent and contemporary Anglo-Saxons, the modern business corporation is analogous to the "proposition nation" concept: merely a concatenation of contracts, with no ethnic character, although Fraser is quick to note that corporations dominated by other groups do not lose their ethnic character.

The American Revolution is still "a work in progress." There have been three transformations thus far: the Constitutional Republic dating from the American Revolution to the Civil War and based on political decentralization, liberty, and egalitarianism; the Bourgeois Republic resulting from the victory of the North in the Civil War and lasting until FDR, typified by the 14th Amendment and a large increase in federal power; and the Managerial/Therapeutic leviathan since that period, characterized by even greater concentration of power at the federal level, combined now with energetic attempts to change the attitudes of Americans in a liberal and eventually in an Anglophobic direction. None of these were explicitly Anglo-Saxon Protestant: even at the outset, "the Anglo-Saxon character of the Constitutional Republic was merely *implicit*" [emphasis in original]. The fourth, as yet unrealized, republic is slated to be the Transnational Republic where all traces of White domination have been erased and WASPs have become "a shrinking and despised minority."

[168]

For Fraser, the leveling, egalitarian tendencies of the Constitutional Republic went much too far because they fundamentally opposed the aristocratic Indo-European tripartite model which resulted in a leisured aristocracy:

> *A natural social order dating from time out of mind had been leveled. The egalitarian sense that every free man must participate in labor now outlawed "invidious" social distinctions between those who worked, those who prayed, and those who fought.*

It also aggravated the growing split between the North and South. Both the celebration of work and the disparagement of idleness made "the South with its leisured aristocracy supported by slavery even more anomalous than it had been at the time of the Revolution." Combined with the anti-institutional fervor of evangelical revivalism, the democratic ideology of free labor eventually lent its mass appeal to a multi-pronged crusade against Negro slavery. . . . The conquest and destruction of the Old South marked the second phase of the permanent American Revolution.

The triumph of the North in the Civil War meant that the U.S. was even further removed from its Indo-European roots than before. Congruent with his sympathies for the aristocratic culture of the South as far more compatible with traditional Indo-European social organization, Fraser is unapologetic about slavery: "Not only could a strong scriptural case be made in favor of slavery but a strict construction of the Constitution also favored the pro-slavery argument."

[169]

The result of Lincoln's victory was that limits on federal power "were swept aside by executive decree and military might."

By crushing the southern states, Lincoln fatally weakened the federal principle; his arbitrary exercise of emergency powers laid the foundations for executive dictatorship whenever exceptional circumstances justify the suspension of constitutional liberties. The war was an exercise in constitutional duplicity; the ratification of the Fourteenth Amendment in 1868 was accomplished only by means of blatant fraud and military coercion. Nonetheless, once securely enshrined in the Constitution, the amendment provided both the Second [i.e., Bourgeois] Republic and the Third [i.e., Managerial/Therapeutic] Republic with their formal constitutional warrant. ... By the standard of the First (Federal) Republic, the Fourteenth Amendment was unconstitutional. But, despite some initial resistance, the legal priesthood of the Republic soon elevated the amendment to the status of sacred writ.

[170]

Following the Civil War, there were disagreements among elite Anglo-Saxon intellectuals on race and the ability to successfully absorb the former slaves. For the race realists, Fraser emphasizes William Graham Sumner, a social Darwinist, who thought that social class divisions and competition were part of the natural order of things. Writing in 1903, he noted that "the two races live more independently of each other now than they did" during the slave era. But during the same period, self-styled WASP "progressives," like Supreme Court Justice John Harlan, "labored ceaselessly to promote the egalitarian myth of the color-blind constitution."

This was also the period when immigrants from eastern and southern Europe were flooding the country, threatening to change its identity. For a time, at least, the forces of Anglo-Saxon ethnic defense, spearheaded by New England intellectuals like Madison Grant, Lothrop Stoddard, and Edward A. Ross in alliance with the South and West, won out, culminating in the short-lived victory of the immigration law of 1924.

Fraser sees the Managerial/Therapeutic Republic as flatly unconstitutional. The original constitution has been jettisoned to the point that it has no relationship to the actual structure and operation of the federal government. A new managerial class, first described by James Burnham, had come to power. The result is a "multiracialist managerial revolution" that is "an explicitly post-Christian civil religion; a free-floating *Constitutionalism* has displaced the implicitly Anglo-Saxon *Protestantism* of the first 'white man's country.' Since the New Deal...the myth of the Constitution has been severed from its biocultural roots in Anglo-Saxon Christendom." Anglo-Saxons have abdicated their leading role to a rainbow coalition of groups, including Jews, Blacks, and Catholics, feminists, and homosexuals.

[171]

In Part Three, Fraser concludes with his prescription for the future of Anglo-Saxons. While acknowledging the difficulty of the task, Fraser hopes that WASPs will rediscover themselves as an ethno-nation by rallying around a redefined British monarchy and the Christian tradition: Crown, Church, and Country. Following 18th-century political philosopher Henry St. John, Viscount of Bolingbroke, Fraser advocates a "Patriot King come to deliver them from evil, seizing victory from the jaws of defeat." The king will be a living icon, inspiring but without real power. He envisions a diaspora where the Anglo-Saxons are given formal recognition as a group and are able to form their own autonomous institutions with "binding norms of in-group solidarity"—in effect governing themselves as traditional Jewish diaspora groups (i.e., Orthodox and Hasidic Jews) have always done. As with Jewish groups, the result would be a global network—a network that will be indispensable in what Fraser sees as a "New Dark Age" of global disorder about to engulf the world. This impending "Long Emergency" of "catastrophe and collapse" can only be negotiated by groups with strong ethnic and cultural ties and a willingness to engage in within-group altruism. In this new age, the Anglican Church will play a central role: "The next Protestant Reformation must recall the Anglican Church to its original mission to shepherd the Anglo-Saxon race into the Kingdom of God."

[172]

Fraser has done an extraordinary job in charting the outline and key turning points in the history of the Anglo-Saxons, and the decline of the West more generally. I agree with Frank Salter, whose comments are reproduced on the cover, that Fraser provides "a fresh analysis of the ethno-religious foundations of the English people.... Agree or disagree with Andrew Fraser's prescriptions, his combination of originality and scholarship deserves to find a place in literature dealing with ethnicity, nationalism, constitutional history, biosocial science, and advocacy for Anglo-Saxon ethnic identity and biocultural continuity. Be prepared to read, reread, and ponder."

What follows are some of my own ponderings.

§

THE NON-UNITARY ETHNIC BASIS OF ANGLO-SAXONS

I agree with Fraser that the fundamental break in the history of the Anglo-Saxons is the rise of the Puritans and the overthrow of the primeval Indo-European social order in England, to be followed eventually by other European societies. Fraser correctly notes the strong egalitarian tendencies of the Puritans. As noted elsewhere[7], however, these egalitarian tendencies are far more compatible with the hunter-gatherer model of European origins than the Indo-European warrior elite model. So the question is where these strong egalitarian tendencies came from. My proposal is that these tendencies toward egalitarian individualism, which characterize the peoples of Europe, particularly northern Europe, date from the Ice Ages and existed prior to the Indo-European invasions in the 4th millennium BC. This analysis is compatible with relatively small income- and social-class differences characteristic of Scandinavian society throughout its history, including the absence of serfdom during the Middle Ages—a pattern that reflects a hunter-gatherer model far more than an aristocratic model.

[173]

---

[7]   Kevin MacDonald, "Review of Ricardo Duchesne's The Uniqueness of Western Civilization." *The Occidental Quarterly*, Vol. 11 (3), Fall, 2011, 47-74.

Fraser is certainly aware of differences among the Anglo-Saxons—he several times cites David Hackett Fischer's classic *Albion's Seed: Four British Folkways in America*[8]; but he does not see them as ethnic differences. In this regard it is noteworthy that, as Fischer notes, the elitist, hierarchical model of the West Saxons was already apparent in southwest England dating from at least the 9th century. This group had large estates with lower-middle class *servi and villani*—essentially slaves.

As Fraser notes, the perception of the newly liberated classes after the English Revolution was that "Old England had been steeped in slavery," and they had no desire to return to that. It is easy to romanticize the tripartite Indo-European social form, but the problem is that the aristocratic model did result in exploitation, and "those who worked" often reasonably resented the powers and riches of "those who fought" and their oftentimes unholy alliance with "those who prayed."

[174]

My view is that the Puritans exemplify the egalitarian-individualist trend of Western society dating from before the imposition of the Indo-European model tripartite model. As Fraser is well aware, Puritan culture does not at all fit the warrior elite model. Puritans produced "a civic culture of high literacy, town meetings, and a tradition of freedom," distinguished from other British groups by their "comparatively large ratios of

---

[8]   David Hackett Fischer, *Albion's Seed: Four British Folkways in America* (Oxford, UK: Oxford University Press, 1989).

freemen and small numbers of *servi and villani*[9]—phenomena quite the opposite of the Indo-European aristocratic model. These patterns date from Anglo-Saxon prehistory.

One may deplore the passing of the aristocratic model, as Fraser does, but it's quite clear that in any case, one must attempt to understand the dominant Puritan influence on WASP culture as a pre-condition for an analysis of contemporary WASP pathology. Briefly, my take is that this subgroup is highly intelligent (*e.g.*, they established Harvard and other elite universities shortly after arriving in America), innovative (as Charles Murray shows[10], inventors derived from the northern European peoples are responsible for a hugely disproportionate number of the important inventions that define the modern era), and capable of producing high-trust societies based on individual reputation rather than kinship relationships. Fraser deplores their materialism, their rational approach to the world, and their concern with worldly success. He is quite correct that in the absence of a strong sense of ethnic cohesion and loyalty, these traits certainly become components of ethnic suicide; but they resulted in extraordinarily successful economies that have been the envy of the world.

[175]

---

[9]   Kevin Phillips, *Cousins' Wars: Religion, Politics, Civil Warfare and the Triumph of Anglo-America* (New York: Basic Books, 1999), 26. See also MacDonald, "Review of Ricardo Duchesne's *The Uniqueness of Western Civilization*."

[10] Charles Murray, *Human Accomplishment: The Pursuit of Excellence in the Arts and Sciences, 800 B.C. to 1950* (New York: Harper Perennial, 2004).

Whereas the aristocratic-egalitarian military group was based on the *comitatus* model emphasizing cohesion and loyalty as a result of fealty to a successful leader, the Puritan model for cohesion was the creation of a morally defined in-group.[11] These two models are thus variants on the individualist theme. The Puritans famously imposed penalties on people who departed from the moral/ideological strictures of the society. Puritan "ordered liberty" was the freedom to act within the confines of the moral order. This might be called the "paradox of individualism": In order to form cohesive groups, individualists have at times erected strong social controls on individual behavior in order to promote group cohesion. They were also willing to incur great costs to impose their moral/ideological version of truth: Puritans were prone to "altruistic punishment,"[12] defined as punishment of people who depart from the moral-ideological consensus that costs the punisher. And for the secular-minded descendants of the Puritans in the 19th century, slavery and the aristocratic model of Southern society were anathema to the point that their destruction warranted huge sacrifices.

[176]

The logic connecting these tendencies to the individualist hunter-gather model is obvious: Like all humans in a dangerous and difficult world, hunter-gatherers need to develop cohesive, cooperative ingroups. But rather than base

---

[11] Kevin MacDonald, "American Transcendentalism: An Indigenous Culture of Critique." *The Occidental Quarterly* vol. 8, Summer 2008, 91-106.

[12] E. Fehr & S. Gächter, "Altruistic Punishment in Humans," *Nature* 415, 2002, 137-140.

them on known kinship relations, the prototypical egalitarian-individualist groups of the West are based on reputation and trust. Egalitarian-individualists create moral-ideological communities in which those who violate public trust and other manifestations of the moral order are shunned, ostracized, and exposed to public humiliation—a fate that would have resulted in evolutionary death during the harsh ecological period of the Ice Age—the same fate as the derelict father who refused to provision his children.

The point here, and I am sure that Fraser would agree, is that the culture of the West as it developed in the modern era owes much more to the egalitarian individualism model of the Puritans than to the Indo-European model of aristocratic individualism.

[177]

BEYOND PURITANS AND CAVALIERS

Fraser is certainly aware of differences among different WASP groups, and thus far, the discussion has emphasized the Cavalier-descended Southern aristocratic culture and the Puritan-descended elite that became dominant, especially after the Civil War. Besides these groups, David Hackett Fischer discusses two other British groups: the Quakers, who are even more universalist and egalitarian than the Puritans, but nowhere near as culturally influential or economically dominant; and the Scots-Irish, who came from Northern England, Ulster, and the lowlands of Scotland. This group had a great deal of influence on culture of the American South and West. Fraser is surely right that the Puritan-descended WASP elite that dominated the board rooms and the elite universities have lost their religious faith, and what is left of it is little more than a mild version of cultural Marxism; they have generally succumbed to the destructive forces of the new cultural dispensation. This is not the case with the descendants of the Scots-Irish. Fischer describes their "prevailing cultural mode as profoundly conservative and xenophobic";[13] historically, they detested both the Cavalier-descended planters and the Puritan-descended abolitionists. "In the early twentieth century they would become intensely negrophobic and antisemitic. In our own time they are furiously hostile to both communists and capitalists."

[178]

There is some indication that they were less individualistic than other groups originating in England: to an extent far greater than their Puritan co-ethnics, they were more involved in clan relationships of extended families rather than merely lineal descent. "Marriage ties were weaker than blood ties," and there was a tendency to marry within the extended family—both markers of greater collectivism.

The Scots-Irish certainly have not lost their faith. They showed "intense hostility to organized churches and established clergy on the one hand and [an] abiding interest in religion on the other." They rejected the Anglican Church, religious taxes, and established clergy, but for all that, they were intensely and emotionally religious. Indeed, this group is the main force behind the culture of the American Bible Belt—the religious fundamentalism

[13]   Fischer, *Albion's Seed, Ibid.*

that is such an important aspect of contemporary American politics. They are, indeed, socially conservative and a great many of them are involved in the angry protests of the Tea Party movement. They are the epitome of implicit Whiteness,[14] flocking to White cultural events like NASCAR racing and gun shows.

The problem is that, along with the rest of White America, they are channelled by the media, federal government, legal system, and their own religious leaders to be silent on the matter of race; moreover, quite often their brand of evangelical religion is decidedly pro-Israel, which makes them avid supporters of the foreign-policy programs of the Israel lobby and the Republican Party (as defined by the Jewish dominated "neoconservatives.") Nevertheless, this group of WASPs is likely to be a thorn in the side of the elites well into the future.

[179]

RATIONALITY

Fraser deplores the rationalist tendencies of WASP culture because they ultimately undermined religion and ultimately the Anglo-Saxon ethno-nation.[15] Thus, Fraser sees scholastic philosophy, which was heavily influenced by Aristotle, as leading to "the divorce of God from man." Darwin's "bleak and disenchanted vision" was simply the endpoint of a centuries-long

---

[14] Kevin MacDonald, "Psychology and White Ethnocentrism." *The Occidental Quarterly*, vol. 6 (4), Winter, 2006-07, 7-46.

[15] See. Kevin MacDonald, "Neoconservatism as a Jewish Movement," *The Occidental Quarterly*, vol. 4, Summer 2004, 1-18; "The Neoconservative Mind." *The Occidental Quarterly*, vol. 8 (3), Fall 2008, 1-18.

process that displaced God from the Western mind, rendering Westerners defenseless against the onslaught of other peoples.

However, I would argue that the rationality of Anglo-Saxons is just as fundamental as the irrational, emotional and religious aspects. As Ricardo Duchesne points out, one aspect of European uniqueness originated with the Greeks, who invented scientific reasoning by offering explanations of natural events that were entirely general. Duchesne defends Max Weber's claim that, far more than any other civilization, the West exhibited a greater level of rationalization of all aspects of life. He comments on the greater extent to which "social activities involving the calculation of alternate means to a given end were rationalized, and in the higher degree to which *theoretical* beliefs about the nature of the universe, life, and God were rationalized through the use of definitions, theorems, and concepts."[16]

[180]

There are deep relationships between rationality and individualism: individualists are prone to seeing the world in universalist terms, objectively and without biases resulting from in-group allegiances. This accounts for the strong tendency for moral universalism in Western philosophy, and as Weber notes, this rationalistic stance predisposes the West to create rational bureaucracies "managed by specialized and trained officials in accordance with impersonal and universal statuses and regulations formulated and recorded in writing."[17]

---

[16] Duchesne, *The Uniqueness of Western Civilization*, 248.

[17] *Ibid.*, 249

It is certainly the case that this proneness to universalism and rationalism can result in failure to defend the legitimate particularlistic ethnic interests of the West in the name of universalist ideals. That is, indeed, what we are seeing now. However, there is no question that particularist ethnic interests are defensible from a rational, scientific perspective.[18]

Indeed, the WASP ethnic defense of the 1920s, resulting in the Immigration Restriction Law of 1924, was energized partly by an intellectual understanding of Darwinism and race, not by a religious sensibility. The strong emphasis on rationality meant that public discourse on immigration policy in the 1920s necessarily took place in an atmosphere where scientific ideas and rational discourse had pride of place. The basic argument of the restrictionists was that all groups in the country had legitimate interests in retaining their share of the national population, including Whites (or, more accurate in the case of Madison Grant and the eugenicists, *Nordics*).[19]

[181]

Nevertheless, for Fraser, the rational basis of the WASP ethnic defense was why it ultimately failed:

> *Lost altogether was the primordial understanding that Anglo-Saxon identity is inseparable from the blood faith of a Christian people. Once American political theology fell under the influence of*

---

[18] Frank Salter, *On Genetic Interests*.

[19] Kevin MacDonald, *The Culture of Critique* (Westport, CT: Praeger, 1998), Chapter 7.

*scientific modernism, racial realists lost interest
in the ethnoreligious traditions of Anglo-Saxon
Christendom. . . . Scientific racism... bore the
stamp of a soulless and self-defeating materialism.
Racial realism was too cold and aloof to regenerate
a sense of ethnoreligious solidarity among Anglo-
Saxon Protestants. It left middle-class Americans
unable to decide whether they were simply whites,
or one of several more exotic breeds such as the
Nordics, Aryans, or Caucasians. Lacking firm roots
in the historical literature and popular culture
of a folk religion, in ancestral myths of heroism,
chivalry, and romantic love, Anglo-Saxon racial
solidarity had little purchase within the collective
machinery of social control that increasingly
governed industrial America.*

[182]

The WASP ethnic defense doubtless had emotional
roots (more apparent in the non-Puritan-descended Anglo-
Saxons of the West and South), but it was justified in a scientific,
rational manner. The ultimate defeat of the WASP ethnic defense
occurred because of the rise of the "Culture of Critique"—
particularly Boasian anthropology, the Frankfurt School, and
the general academic culture of the left.

*It is probable that the decline in evolutionary and
biological theories of race and ethnicity facilitated
the sea change in immigration policy brought
about by the 1965 law. As Higham (1984) notes,
by the time of the final victory in 1965, which
removed national origins and racial ancestry from
immigration policy and opened up immigration*

to all human groups, the Boasian perspective of cultural determinism and anti-biologism had become standard academic wisdom. The result was that "it became intellectually fashionable to discount the very existence of persistent ethnic differences. The whole reaction deprived popular race feelings of a powerful ideological weapon" (Higham 1984, 58-59). Jewish intellectuals were prominently involved in the movement to eradicate the racialist ideas of Grant and others.[20]

In other words, the failure of WASP ethnic defense occurred because the high ground in rational, scientific debate had been seized by Jews as ethnic competitors. Note also John Higham's point that the intense emotions felt by the restrictionists eventually failed because of the failure of restrictionist science. In the absence of an intellectually legitimate grounding, the WASP ethnic defense was doomed.

[183]

This is an incredibly important object lesson for contemporary attempts to defend White interests: We must be able to seize the rational, scientific high ground because that is essential to public debate in Western societies and ultimately to the emotional commitment of Whites to a sense of having group interests as Whites—in other words, to their very survival. In my view, a well-grounded scientific understanding of White genetic

---

[20] MacDonald, *The Culture of Critique*, 252-253. The inner quotations are to: Carl Degler, *In Search of Human Nature: The Decline and Revival of Darwinism in American Social Thought* (Oxford and New York: Oxford University Press, 1991); John Higham, *Send These to Me: Immigrants in Urban America*, rev. ed. (Baltimore: Johns Hopkins University Press, 1984).

interests that rationalizes the intense natural motives of ethnic affiliation is likely to be far more effective in rallying Whites, especially elite Whites, than religious feelings. As Fraser is all too well aware, the story of religious feeling in the modern age has been to either sink into irrelevance for secular Whites (who are likely to be more educated) or be diverted into causes that are suicidal for religious Whites.

JEWISH INFLUENCE

[184]

Fraser is quite aware of the ethnocentric aspect of Judaism and Jewish hostility toward Christianity. Indeed, I agree with his comment that "for most Jews. . . inveterate hostility toward Christianity is more important to their collective identity than 'solidarity with Israel.'" Moreover, Fraser is not unaware of Jewish influence. He has a nice comment on Felix Adler's universalist Ethical Culture society which promoted Anglo-Saxon cosmopolitanism and ethnic disappearance while promising that Jews would lose their ethnic coherence only after everyone else had done so. This sentiment—actually a mainstream ideology among Reform Jews of the period—would put off the sacrifice of their own ethnicity until "the arrival of a 'post-ethnic' utopia." He credits them as "major players in the design and execution of the new constitutional order" underlying the New Deal. He also has a nice section of the Jewish campaign to rid the public square of any trace of Christianity.

Fraser also asks whether the abdication of the WASP has really resulted in a better society now that it is dominated by "an increasingly corrupt corporate plutocracy in which Ivy League Jews are heavily over-represented.... Worse still, Jewish elites harbor a deep-seated animus toward the Christian faith professed by most Americans." And he notes the hypocrisy whereby "the Jewish civil religion explicitly disallows the desire of both Anglo-Saxon Protestants and ethnic Catholics to live in predominantly European Christian societies. At the same time organized Jewry loudly insists that Israel's character as an explicitly Jewish state must be preserved and protected." Moreover, Fraser notes that "ethnocentric Jewish elites bear a large, unacknowledged (but glaringly obvious, to those with eyes to see) share of responsibility" for militant Islam, moral decline, financial collapse and economic depression.

[185]

Nevertheless, he fails to deal with the Culture of Critique—Jewish intellectual domination, their very large influence on the media and the political process, and their role in promoting massive immigration of non-Whites which, after all, is the root of the entire problem.[21] As noted above, the triumph of the Jewish intellectual elite after WWII spelled the death knell of the WASP ethnic defense that culminated in the immigration law of 1924. The organized Jewish community was also pivotal in promoting massive non-White immigration beginning with their triumph of the 1965 immigration law. WASPs indeed have their weaknesses. But in the absence of the rise of a hostile Jewish

[21]   MacDonald, *The Culture of Critique.*

elite, there is no reason to suppose that America would now be confronted with 100,000,000 non-Whites, many harboring historical grudges against Whites, and under threat to have a non-White majority in the foreseeable future.[22]

WHITES VERSUS WASPS

Fraser's appeal is to WASPs, not the "dangerously over-inclusive racial phenotype" of White. But, as he notes, "in the first 'white man's country,' age-old ethnic differences between English, Scotch-Irish, Scots, Welsh, German and French Huguenot colonists literally paled into insignificance." Fraser argues that the concept of Whiteness "always implied the inherent equality of anyone passing" for White, a logic that repelled conservatives, who were attracted to the talented members of other races and capitalists who cared more about the cost of their workers than their race. Fraser advises WASPs to shed the label of "White" in favor of "reasserting their ancestral identity as Anglo-Saxons."

[186]

I do think that different White subgroups should continue to remain separate, particularly in Europe where it would be a very large loss to lose the different languages and cultures of the various European groups. Even in the United States, it is nice to

[22] See my review of Eric P. Kaufmann's *The Rise and Fall of Anglo-America*; *The Occidental Observer*, July 29, 2009, accessed May 1, 2012, http://www.theoccidentalobserver.net/articles/MacDonald-Kaufmann.html.

see celebrations of Scottish, Irish, and other European cultures by their descendants.

However, it would be foolish indeed to organize politically solely on the basis of these sub-groups. The term "White" in the American political context refers to all 200 million people of European descent—a very large and politically powerful group, whereas the descendants of Anglo-Saxon Protestants are a much smaller group. The obvious strategy is to legitimize a sense of White identity and White interests in the current climate, dominated as it is by elites hostile to the traditional White peoples and White culture of America. Having an identity *qua* White need not compromise identifications with sub-groups of Whites. There are important differences among these groups, as emphasized in this review. However, we are all quite closely related—indeed, Europeans are the most genetically homogeneous continental group on Earth. And we should all have a sense of our common cultural heritage, spanning from the Classical Age to the Italian Renaissance to German Romanticism to the English drama.

[187]

Such a rational construction of our ethnic interests in the contemporary world is therefore not without a strong biological basis of near kinship, but also carries with it an intense emotional appreciation of the common European culture and its accomplishments. My hope is that these two strands can eventually win the day, despite the current very large threat to our people and culture. ೩०●

The

SPINOZA
STRATEGY

PAUL DEUSSEN

*The heretical Right
must learn the art
of writing under
persecution—that
of subverting a
dominant ideology
from the inside.*

PAUL DEUSSEN
is a doctoral student in the
humanities.

[*image*]
"Baruch de Spinoza"
Portrait (c. 1665)
Gemäldesammlung der
Herzog-August-Bibliothek
Wikimedia

Challenging

orthodoxy has always been a dangerous affair. The unorthodox Right—European nationalist, Traditionalist, the "alternative Right" writ large—often complains about the censorship, name-calling, and character assassinations we endure for writing seriously about race and culture; however, if we take a step back for a moment and consider the persecution suffered by those who challenged the religious orthodoxy, our struggle seems pleasant by comparison. Burnings at the stake, beatings in the street, and public executions were but a few of the tactics employed by the Church to silence those who questioned the unquestionable. Perhaps then, it would behoove us to take a closer look at the strategy of those who successfully challenged— and eventually *defeated*—religious orthodoxy under these life-threatening conditions. We may dislike much about the world that arose in the aftermath of the Enlightenment, but we can still admire and learn from the strategy employed by its early partisans.

A useful place to begin would be Baruch Spinoza (1632-1677), who is considered by many political theorists to be the father of modern liberal democracy. Surrounded by controversy throughout much of his life, Spinoza was one of the most radical philosophers of the modern period. He possessed a remarkable talent for provoking people to question basic assumptions and values; his willingness to challenge religious particularism resulted in, among other things, his excommunication from the Jewish community in 1656. Such a punishment seemed entirely justified in the eyes of 19th-century Jewish philosophers like Hermann Cohen. However, the 20th-century political philosopher Leo Strauss (1899-1973) came to Spinoza's defense in his *Spinoza's Critique of Religion*, in which he wrote that

[192]   much of the hostile condemnation directed towards Spinoza was caused by a misunderstanding of his thought and strategy. Strauss believed that in a world dominated by the Church, attacking Judaism was a shrewd way for Spinoza to lay siege to Christianity, his ultimate target.

If subterfuge is the name of the game, then Spinoza was truly one of its masters.

The starting point of Spinoza's philosophy is that man is ultimately responsible for his own fate. He rejected the belief of Maimonides (1135-1204) that God was a rational being, arguing instead that if God were truly omnipotent, then God would have the power to be exactly what he wanted to be (rational, arational, or otherwise). And if God could recreate himself, then so could man, which meant Spinoza also rejected the concept of evil, because "the evil passions are evil only with a view to human utility. . . "[1]

In other words, the things men considered to be wicked or immoral were merely problems that could be managed and eventually overcome. Spinoza's ardent belief in progress and the potential of mankind to correct the evils of human behavior would ultimately lay the groundwork for the modern liberal state, but he could only do this, as Strauss demonstrates, by showing "the way toward a new religion or religiousness which was to inspire a wholly new kind of society, a new kind of Church."[2]

To accomplish this task, Spinoza wrote his *Theologico-Political Treatise* in which he used a bait-and-switch technique of attacking Judaism in order to lead his Christian readers into a general critique of *all* religions.

[193]

The Jewish philosopher Hermann Cohen (1842-1918) strongly opposed the work of Spinoza and charged him with conceiving of the state "entirely in terms of power politics, divorced from religion and morality, thus rendering the state above religion."[3]

Cohen also indicted Spinoza for denying that the God of Israel was the God of all mankind and for reducing Jewish religion

---

[1]   Leo Strauss, *Jewish Philosophy and the Crisis of Modernity* (New York, NY: SUNY Press, 1997), 157.

[2]   *Ibid.,* 156.

[3]   *Ibid.,* 158.

to a doctrine of the Jewish state. The former was blasphemy and the latter served to diminish the Torah to human origin, both of which rendered Spinoza blind to biblical prophecy and hence to the core of Judaism. Cohen also believed Spinoza's critique of the Jewish religion to be ripe with contradictions. For instance, it made little sense to single out the Mosaic Law as the suppressing force of philosophy, when it was unclear that Jesus Christ himself championed the freedom of philosophy. But what may have incensed Cohen the most about Spinoza's *Treatise* was the claim that Mosaic Law was particularistic and tribal and served no other end than the earthly or political felicity of the Jewish nation. In this regards, the moral implications of Spinoza's religious transgressions were far less damning than his disloyalty to the Jewish people. Cohen believed Spinoza deserved nothing less than excommunication because he gave comfort and aid to the enemies of the Jews by first idealizing Christianity and then indulging in every Christian prejudice against Judaism.

[194]

The vitriol with which Cohen condemned Spinoza was impressive and should be all too familiar to the unorthodox Right. He regarded the defector's behavior as "unnatural" and a "humanly incomprehensible act of treason." To act this way, Spinoza must have been a disturbed man "possessed by an evil demon." Cohen's criticism is reminiscent of the frequent diatribes against "racists" as vile and mentally deformed creatures in need of sensitivity training, if not medication.

Leo Strauss's interpretation of Spinoza's behavior discounted the self-hating Jew explanation and suggested that Cohen had not paid "sufficient attention to the harsh necessity to which Spinoza bowed by writing in the manner in which he wrote."[4] Heresy and blasphemy of Christianity were offenses punishable by death, which deterred most philosophers from directly challenging the Church. Jews in particular felt this intimidation because they were haunted by the experience of the Spanish Inquisition.

But Strauss did not believe the deterrent factor alone explained Spinoza's decision to single out Judaism. Instead, Spinoza seemed to be employing a carefully thought-out strategy to reach a wider audience with a message that could be absorbed, internalized, and expanded upon . . . and that would lead his audience towards a greater truth. Put bluntly, Spinoza's purpose was to show mankind the way towards a liberal society and his strategy was one of subterfuge.

[195]

Spinoza was writing for a devoted Christian audience and thus had to modify his message accordingly. This meant playing off their anti-Semitic prejudices and urging them to free "spiritual Christianity from all carnal Jewish relics,"[5] like the resurrection of the body. By making the Old Testament the scapegoat for everything he found objectionable in Christianity, Spinoza presented his general argument against religious

---

[4]   *Ibid.*, 166.

[5]   *Ibid.*, 160.

particularism in a form that was palatable to Christians (i.e., in an anti-Semitic fashion). To be clear, his disparagement of Judaism and the Mosaic Law was not insincere. Spinoza was striving to create a new universal religion for both Jews and Christians, and he also believed Jews had more to overcome to get there, since, as Strauss relates, "Moses' religion is a political law" and "to adhere to his religion as he proclaimed it is incompatible with being the citizen of any other state."[6] Cohen's misunderstanding was to think that Spinoza wanted the eradication of religious devotion to end with Judaism. In other words, he failed to follow Spinoza's thought that freedom of philosophy required a liberal state that was neither Christian nor Jewish. The Jews may have had to be liberated from Judaism—but the Christians also had to be liberated from Christianity.

In the *Introduction to Persecution and the Art of Writing*, Strauss gives an excellent accounting of this argumentation style as it was advocated by the Islamic philosopher Farabi.[7] Farabi (c. 872-950) said that when Socrates was confronted with the decision to conform to what he held to be false opinions and the wrong ways of life of his fellow citizens, he stubbornly chose non-conformity—and was punished with death. Farabi believed this may have been the suitable choice in dealing with the elite, but it was ill-advised to attempt this approach with the vulgar. Dealings with the common man required a strategy styled on Plato, that is, gradually replacing accepted opinions with the truth, or an

---

[6]   *Ibid.*

[7]   *Ibid.*, 424.

approximation of the truth—changing minds by provisionally accepting conventional wisdom. More specifically, and as it applies to the Spinoza example, Farabi believed that "conformity with the opinions of the religious community in which one is brought up is a necessary qualification for the future philosopher."

The strategy outlined above should not be understood simply in terms of avoiding persecution, because what is really at issue here may be the best method of philosophy. If you want to reach the most people with your message in a way that you can actually change their minds about something, the new truth you are presenting cannot flagrantly contradict their sacrosanct beliefs. In other words, when challenging orthodoxy in any form, it is always prudent to *signal towards the orthodoxy* before *turning towards radicalism*. Appearing loyal and loving to what is already loved—and then transforming it from within—is far more effective than challenging it head-on. This is philosophy at the highest level, where the means of delivery are as important as the message being delivered.

[197]

In a discussion of Niccolo Machiavelli's rhetorical strategy in *The Prince*—which Strauss considers equally damaging to the Judeo-Christian worldview, albeit in different ways, as Spinoza's *oeuvre*—Strauss writes that Machiavelli's most radical ideas are never explicit, but presented through implication:

> *When a man openly utters or vomits a blasphemy,*
> *all good men shudder and turn away from him,*

or punish him according to his deserts; the sin is entirely his. But a concealed blasphemy is so insidious, not only because it protects the blasphemer against punishment by due process of law, but above all because it practically compels the hearer or reader to think the blasphemy by himself and thus to become an accomplice of the blasphemer. Machiavelli thus establishes a kind of intimacy with his readers par excellence, whom he calls "the young," by inducing them to think forbidden or criminal thoughts. Such an intimacy seems also to be established by every prosecutor or judge who, in order to convict the criminal, must think criminal thoughts, but that intimacy is abhorred by the criminal. Machiavelli, however, intends it and desires it. This is an important part of his education of the young or, to use the time-honored expression, of his corruption of the young.[8]

[198]

It should be of particular interest to the unorthodox Right that signaling one way and turning the other was the strategy used by the egalitarians when they convinced the Western world to embrace racial equality. Had the Boas cult simply declared the racial beliefs of Western man to be immoral and completely unfounded, their arguments would have fallen on deaf ears. What they did instead was moderate their position with the claim that all perceived inequalities among the races

---

[8]   Leo Strauss, "Niccolo Machiavelli," *History of Political Philosophy,* Leo Strauss and Joesph Cropsey (eds.) (Chicago and London: University of Chicago Press, 1963), 312-313.

were caused by variances in culture. This concession earned Boas and his followers the trust of their target audience because it soothed Western man's pride, conformed to his prejudices, and did not encumber him with charges of racial injustice. Cultural inequality actually placed the burden of responsibility on minorities who needed to get their act together by adopting Western man's superior way of life. Boas and his followers probably never really believed this, but they had to make a tactical settlement in order to be heard, which is to say, they had to appear loyal to Western civilization before they could get any traction challenging its long-held assumption of racial inequality. What followed next is well-known to most readers of this publication. Having convinced their audience to take this initial step towards equality, the egalitarians became far more ambitious in pursuing their true revolutionary agenda.

[199]

What the unorthodox Right can learn from Spinoza—and Boas—is a strategy of subterfuge. If we desire to reach audiences beyond the readers of this publication, then we must understand, as Spinoza and Boas did, that the gradual replacement of sacrosanct ideas has to be accompanied by a provisional acceptance of the conventional wisdom of our time. In other words, we must be willing to signal left before turning right. Only then will we be able to reach wider audiences in a way that might provoke them to question the unquestionable. It is probably asking a lot of us to appear loyal to, let alone adoring of, the gods of multiculturalism, diversity, and equality, but employing such a strategy when writing for politically correct audiences would be far more effective than directly challenging orthodoxy.

One such tactic might be to support some of the ideals of the politically correct and then reveal how they are contradicted by others. For example, if the intention of multiculturalism is to preserve the unique cultural identity of minorities in this country, then we could argue that what is really happening is the destruction of diversity by the merging and watering down of cultures into unrecognizable forms. As "true" proponents of diversity, we would be taking the moral high ground in claiming that minority cultures are under siege by "universalism" and "McDonald-ization" and that their preservation can only be achieved through the separation of cultures, not the blending of them together into a homogenous blob. This form of attack would be far more palatable to mainstream audiences than directly confronting multiculturalism with charges of "reverse racism." We could also make the corollary claim that multiculturalism itself is ethno-centric in its origins—i.e. it was invented by White people—and oppressive to minority groups that did not develop a similar ideological standpoint on their own.

[200]

Unfortunately, emphasizing the inherent conflict between multiculturalism and diversity may not always work, since actual global diversity is being preserved by non-Western countries that fear ethnic conflict and do not tolerate immigration or cultural diffusion. The only culture that is being destroyed by multiculturalism is Western culture, a consequence unlikely to trouble "progressive" audiences that reject their heritage and traditions. Moreover, the politically correct are unconcerned about balkanization, since they romantically believe America, the "proposition nation" united by creed, will be spared from the internecine conflicts that ravage other nations. Nevertheless, an argument that multiculturalism is oppressive to minorities and destructive to their organic cultural development could have more traction.

Multiculturalism is often claimed to be a philosophy of pluralism, but the intolerance its followers have for non-believers is a clear indication of its *particularism*. Internalizing this conceptual paradox has been unproblematic for most all PC types. Truly, accepting irreconcilable ideas seem to go hand-in-hand with orthodoxy. Forcing non-believers to convert to multiculturalism is also comfortably sanctioned because the principal subjects of this oppression are Whites. If, however, we [201] can reframe the discussion in such a way that multiculturalism appears to be an ideology forced on minorities to their own detriment, then the reaction from the politically correct would be far different.

The key to bringing down egalitarianism *from the inside* could therefore be the vilification of multiculturalism as a ruling-class conspiracy. Similar to Spinoza who played off the anti-Semite prejudices of Christians, so should we play off the prejudices and neurotic suspicions the politically correct have for Whites. This might be done effectively with class-struggle arguments that link multiculturalism with cheap labor and the exploitation of the Third World by evil White capitalists. A more profound argument could also be made that multiculturalism prevents non-White peoples from achieving their own unique destiny and subordinates them to what Paul Piccone called an abstract universal ideology without meaningful axiological or ontological content.[9] Consequently, minorities are rendered defenseless against the taste manipulations of the culture industry and the social engineering of a managerial bureaucracy that prioritizes rationalism, efficiency, and productivity over traditional and aesthetic ways of life celebrated by non-White peoples. The result is nihilism and moral decadence which must be repressively contained with massive state regulations and control. (This argument also carries the benefit of actually being true). It is more than likely that similar arguments have already been made by vigilantly obsessed members of the Left who are constantly on guard for the injustices of a White cultural hegemony. We should cite these liberal experts, expand upon their arguments, and contribute as much as we can to the reinterpretation of multiculturalism as a racist ideology.

[202]

In other words, to awaken the politically correct from their indoctrinated slumber, we should convincingly accuse them of being guilty of that which they proclaim to be the greatest of sins.

Collapsing the pillar of multiculturalism might not be enough to bring down egalitarianism, but this should be the first step in a protracted campaign of attrition and political subterfuge.

---

[9]   Paul Piccone, "The End of Public Education?" *Telos*, vol. 111 (Spring 1998), 129; "Multicultural Homogenization," *Telos*, vol. 113 (Fall 1998), 187.

For our revolution to be successful, we must be guided by the self-acknowledgement of the weakness of our current position. Tactical settlements have to be made and finding ways to challenge the orthodoxy by signaling left before turning right should become a necessary part of our long-term strategy.

There may come a point, if we are not already there, when egalitarianism becomes so deeply ingrained in our society that it cannot be defeated through outright confrontation. The best way to challenge orthodoxy of this kind will be through its metamorphosis or reshaping. Such a strategy should not be used in a journal such as this one, where we can be honest about our strategies and goals; but we must begin to think beyond our limited reach here and start sending soldiers back into the ranks of the politically correct to bring down the orthodoxy from within.

[203]

The

OLD-TIME
RELIGION

ELIZABETH WRIGHT

*Claiming to be "taking
their country back,"
American conservatives
have, in fact, made a
civic religion of their
own cultural and
spiritual erasure.*

ELIZABETH WRIGHT (1937-2011)

lived a life of self-imposed isolation and obscurity. For those who appreciate her writings, however, she is fondly remembered as one of the most remarkable conservative commentators of her generation. An African-American, and a libertarian and individualist, she nevertheless had a deep understanding of—and "tough love" for—Founding-stock Anglo-Americans. Her greatest insights were, indeed, those of an outsider—one who was out-of-step with the prevailing *Zeitgeist* and could thus view the White race (as well as her own) with critical objectivity.

For more than two decades, Elizabeth was Editor of *Issues and Views*, both in its newsletter and online manifestations. This article was originally published in September 2010 at *Alternative Right*, in response to Glenn Beck's "Restore Honor" rally that had just been held on the Washington, DC, Mall. The piece is a critique of "Tea Party conservatism," which was reaching its culmination at the time (and has since faded). But the essay bursts through this context by virtue of Elizabeth's devastating insights into the psychology of White Americans. The "Tea Party" phenomenon, in her reading, was not simply a reaction to the 2008 stock-market crash or the election of Barack Obama; it was yet one more episode in an ongoing process, in which Europeans gleefully dispossess themselves through their participation in the reigning civic religion.

~ **Richard Spencer**

[*image*]
"Do We Look Racist?"
Glenn Beck "Restore Honor Rally," 28 August 2010
Getty Images

Now that the dust

has settled on that overhyped, fevered Glenn Beck rally, what have we learned? Is it clearer than ever that no sober knight will come riding in to bring the enlightenment that some of us thought the Tea Partiers might have offered? It appears that the expectations surrounding those initial enigmatic stirrings, which made one almost believe that the furor was about more than just anger over political issues, have been extinguished. Was it all just a momentary aberration?

As it turns out, White conservatives don't want to take the lead in preserving what remains of this country's now tenuous White, Anglo-Euro culture. To take on such a responsibility would make them even more vulnerable to the racial bullets and daggers they have been ducking for years.

If Beck's rally taught us anything, it's that nothing has changed in the White middle-class mindset and that fear of the "racist" label continues to rule as strongly as ever. We've now learned for certain that such Whites are determined never to put the name to their fear and anxiety. If anything, they are fighting all the harder to bury even deeper the visceral knowledge of what is going on in this country and the inevitable future that is on its way. Christopher Hitchens's assessment of the August 28 mass meeting is correct, when he claims that Beck's tepid event was "a call to sink to the knees rather than rise from them."[1] (If Hitchens, of all people, gets it, who could miss it?)

[208] Even as other groups gradually dispossess them in the country whose political system was constructed by their forebears, conservative Whites persist in their obstinate assertion that their apparent discontent is "not about race." What hogwash. Of course it's about race and culture. Why shouldn't it be? No matter how assiduously they deny it, resentment is growing over the ever-looming fact that this country, due to swiftly altering demographics, will no longer be the product of those Founders. And reality informs us that the ruling law, that is, the Constitution (or what's left of it), soon will be openly renounced by competing populations that never have had even the remotest historical connection to the notions set forth by those Englishmen.

---

[1]   Christopher Hitchens, "White Fright: Glenn Beck's rally was large, vague, moist, and undirected—the Waterworld of white self-pity." *Slate*, 30 August, 2010, accessed May 1, 2012, http://www.slate.com/ articles/news_and_politics/fighting_words/2010/08/white_fright. html.

No one has to look far abroad to see what is on the horizon. In their guts these conservatives know what's coming, as their unnamed enemies pick up the pace in the drive to usurp political power. What were mere hints just two decades ago have grown into loud trumpet blasts. And along comes Glenn Beck who offers these perceptive, yet reluctant conservatives a way to feel better about things. According to his prescription, all they have to do is Believe and Pray.

After watching that half-baked celebration of Martin Luther King Jr., and the determined laundering of his well-documented leftist convictions, how could one not conclude, like Ross Douthat, that "Beck's "Restoring Honor" was like an Obama rally through the looking glass," that these conservatives wished to be "cosmopolitan and young-at-heart, multicultural and hip"?[2] Nobody wants to be known as "square," whatever squareness entails at any given time. Remember how conservatives used to laugh at and rail at political correctness? Now, they're the ones who don't want to be depicted as "incorrect."

[209]

My observations of these Whites lead me to agree with Paul Gottfried, who astutely argues, "Whites would desert the GOP in droves unless their party continues to make an effort to be PC." And further, he claims, many Republicans would

[2]   Ross Douthat, "Mr. Beck Goes to Washington," *New York Times*, 29 August 2010, accessed May 1, 2012, http://www.nytimes.com/2010/08/30/opinion/30douthat.html?_r=1.

not vote for a party that was "not marching in lockstep with the media in expressing horror over America's evil racist, sexist, and homophobic past."[3]

Whites of all political stripes, no matter which political label they give themselves, have been sold on the unique wickedness of America's past racism that surely had to be the most grievous sin ever committed by mankind. Hence, the Glenn Beck carnival of repentance.

Beck picked up on this peculiar self-flagellation, and his soap opera rally was customized to meet the needs of this constituency. It seems that the unconstitutional *Brown v. Board of Education* court decision, the deceptive Civil Rights Act, forced busing (which tore apart whole school districts around the country), a national holiday for a Black preacher, and endless, ever-evolving new perks and goodies to benefit Black elites, have not quite made the grade of cleansing those past sins.

[210]

And so, to prove that they possess no resentment over the decades of social strife that has plagued our society, in August, the good conservatives took to D.C., where they engaged in a ceremony to worship a 19th-century President, who could come up with no better solution to his nation's problems than a war that brought about the slaughter of hundreds of thousands of his fellow countrymen, and a Black man who specialized in emotional oratory.

---

[3]   Paul Gottfried, "Outreach to Nowhere," AlternativeRight.com, 28 August, 2010, accessed May 1, 2012, http://www.alternativeright.com/ main/blogs/district-of-corruption/the-outreach-to-nowhere/.

One has to wonder who these people are who will march on Washington to "restore" the country's "honor," as the rally's theme boasted, yet are in the forefront of supporting some of the most dishonorable acts engaged in by their country's interchangeable governments. Just what is special about the moral convictions of these advocates, who fervently sermonize on such issues as patriotism, war, family life, religion, the nature of government *ad nauseam*?

On the subject of race, as we've seen, conservatives are savvy on this score and have learned that one way to deflect the scurrilous charge of racism is to celebrate the icons and infinite memorabilia of the civil rights movement, while keeping a contingent of Black people on hand to be prominently displayed at public events. Who said these savvy Whites couldn't be condescending?

[211]

On the other hand, Whites are given little choice in this matter since, at the mere hint of the formation of any kind of all-White entity, Black and liberal elites will come charging in. Even if such an organization is inadvertently all-White, it must first be accused of loathsome, racist motives, so that it can be monitored. No matter how benign the group's objectives, if White men are its creators, then it must be put under surveillance and ultimately neutralized.

When the new group's leaders relent, we find a *quid pro quo* in place—the intruding Blacks get the benefits of prominent positions and other perks, while the Whites now have cover from any other such intrusions and accusations. We saw this game successfully played against the Promise Keepers[4] and, now again, very blatantly applied to the Tea Parties.

The Whites who resent the blackmail flee, while the rest remain comfortably ensconced, adapting to the politically correct reality of the times. Whites, it would seem, must not be left to their own devices. Before taking back the country, is it possible that they will first take back the right to organize among themselves?

But don't feel too sorry, too soon for these conservatives, who greatly influence the country's political direction through the national leaders and ethos they inflict on our society.

[212]

Take a look at how they feel about big government that they rail against so vehemently. It's fine as long as it's out there doing what government should be doing—that means making war. War making, you see, in the mind of the conservative patriot, shows how tough we are. And although we're not supposed to care what the rest of the world thinks of us, it's imperative to earn the world's fearful regard when it comes to our toughness. It matters not who rules in DC, or how many of our young soldiers

---

[4]   The Promise Keepers, a not-for-profit charity, was founded in 1990 by a former Head Football Coach of the University of Colorado, Bill McCartney. His goal was to host mass, all-male religious revivals in football stadiums across America. Much like the Tea Party movement, the Promise Keepers were criticized by feminists as an organization of (overwhelmingly) White men meeting *as men*. Much like the Tea Party, the Promise Keepers had a vague agenda and fell over themselves denouncing racism and pursuing, in McCartney's words, "racial reconciliation."

needlessly die in worthless battles, as long as the message is sent abroad that we're the biggest, baddest country on earth. *We're the USA! USA! USA!*

Conservatives are dedicated to one of their favorite little war slogans, which is designed to justify why our troops are "over there." When Pat Buchanan or Ron Paul comes along and reverses this little ditty, explaining that the terrorists are "over here" only because we're "over there," he gets drummed out of the corps, for "pacifism." Woe to even the most faithful conservative, if he appears to diss the USA's abominable wars of choice.

When Iran's President Ahmadinejad is quoted making negative remarks about the leadership of the United States, primarily due to this country's toadying relationship with Israel, that's reason enough to urge the U.S. military to bomb and kill millions of innocent Iranians. Don't say nasty things about the USA or its Middle East client state, *OR WE'LL KILL YOU!*

[213]

Is this the mentality that worried Founder John Jay, who did not see leaders as being trustworthy initiators of war? In *The Federalist Papers*, he claimed that some leaders will make war even "when their nations are to get nothing by it," and spoke of leaders harboring motives such as "personal ambition, thirst for military glory and revenge for personal affronts." Jay warned about a nation putting itself in situations that "invite hostility or insult," that could lead to "pretended" causes of war. And he was not impressed by the superiority of so-called republics as opposed to monarchies, believing that republics were just as "addicted" to war as monarchies. "Are not the former administered by men as well as the latter?" he asked.

But what did he know? Obviously, not as much as our sanctimonious conservatives, who cheer as 19-year-olds are sent off to prove their mettle, while offering opportunities for these stay-at-home warriors to engage in "support the troops" grandstanding. For all their noisemaking about restoring the Constitution, it is easy to suspect that these impostors look upon the Founders and their document as quaint and outdated as do most liberals.

And who isn't impressed with how well these conservatives have taught us about family and commitment? What outstanding models they have given us. At the moment they are apoplectic over maintaining marriage for opposite sexes only, yet these are the people whose foremost political philosopher, Newt Gingrich, just married his *fourth wife*, making a mockery of that institution. (Will the fifth be the charm?) By the way, this mountebank of "family values" was the fourth husband of his previous wife No. 3. (How many broken vows does that make?) Could homosexuals, who claim to be "married," dilute the significance of marriage any more than this?

Chosen as Leader of the conservative camp by acclamation, this Talking Hero is looked upon as the fount of wisdom to those who seek to teach the rest of us how to think and behave.

These deluded crusaders, in striving to exonerate their other leader by acclamation, Sarah Palin, from the charge of irresponsible parenting, could only shrug and come up with a pithy, new catchphrase: "Life happens." As if we didn't know that. With the advent of Palin, American youth are once again blessed with yet another fine conservative role model.

And what about immigration? Can we really expect to see these conservatives carry through on their stances against illegal immigration? Don't count on it. Is there any chance that today's conservative reformers will take the next step in calling for a moratorium on all immigration, the "legal" kind as well? Is there among some of them, at least, a sense of urgency to stem the tide of endless, unchecked floods from abroad? But then again, is it likely that people who worship at the pedestal of Martin Luther King would understand the meaning of such terms as "cultural suicide" or "death of the West," or care about the transformation that is taking place around them?

[215]

Libya's late leader Muammar Gaddafi used to laugh at the foolish Europeans, who have encouraged the immigration of millions of Third World aliens, and offers Europe's leaders a financial deal to keep more of the mob out of that continent, are American conservatives taking notes?

As literally tens of thousands of African refugees in boats try to reach Italy, the Libyan navy has been instrumental in keeping them out, thanks to an agreement with the Italian government. "We don't know," the bemused Gaddafi is quoted as saying, "if Europe will remain an advanced and united continent or if it will be destroyed, as happened with the barbarian invasions." And then he comes right out and says it: your continent is turning into Africa.

Why should Europe turn into Africa? Why should Europeans want to live in a negrified Europe? Or an Arabized Europe? Why?

The good White conservatives in the U.S., although possessing an instinctive understanding of such questions, would be terrified to entertain such thoughts publicly, or even privately. Better to take one's lead from the huckster Glenn Beck and play it safe, than to express the anxiety to which they dare not put words.

[216]

As one Dutchman observes, "This isn't Holland anymore," nor is it France or England or Germany. And soon it won't be America anymore. In one country after another, clueless Europeans have already begun the process of dispossessing themselves via politics, as immigrants eagerly run for political office, thereby amassing power and influence over the native residents.

Is there something in Europe's water that compels the Whites to submit to this updated form of conquest? Who are voting Black immigrants into political office in Sweden? The native Whites. Who just voted an African into office in Russia? The native Whites. At what point do Whites take responsibility for their ongoing demise or, as Paul Gottfried puts it, for going "soft in the head?"

It is true that, in order to achieve the quasi-religious goals at the heart of the multiculturalists' vision for America, heavy doses of brainwashing have been perpetrated on the public via school systems and throughout the media. The major targets have been youth and, most especially, White youth, as they have had their opinions and beliefs pummeled in "multicultural workshops," and "sensitivity training" sessions. No one can deny that this 30- to 40-year campaign of re-education has been successful.

A recent caller to a New York overnight radio show is almost a stereotype of the proud, de-racinated White man. The de-racinated Zero. He described growing up in Missouri, in the midst of what sounded like a predominantly Anglo population. Years later, when he visited New York City, he claims that this was his first encounter with assertively ethnic people. There he discovered Greek sections of town, Italian sections, Chinese, etc.

[217]

It seems that this did not rest well with him, since he was used to calling himself simply "American," and could not comprehend any reason to expand his ethnic identification with a hyphen. The Zero Man always resents the use of hyphens. Not for him that Greek-American, Italian-American, Polish-American stuff. He's just a plain, old "American," disaffiliated from any specific cultural lineage and expecting everyone else to disaffiliate themselves as well.

This caller sounded as if he would be uncomfortable if described as an "Anglo-American" or "British-American." Mr. Zero probably would be uncomfortable, but why should a Chinese-American attempt to erase his Chinese ancestry to accommodate the deracinated notion of what constitutes an "American?"

The Founders did not seem to think of themselves as Zeros, yet misleading hype continues the fiction that this country was formed in a vacuum by people who shared no heritage. If this were so, why did John Jay thank Providence for giving this country to "one united people," who were "descended from the same ancestors?" Who establishes anything, that is expected to take root, with someone else's progeny in mind?

[218]

Western countries are now being inundated with populations of foreigners who actively discourse on who they are, and they're not going to let you forget it. As masses of Muslims bring their distinctive customs, laws and disciplines to Christian countries, and push the envelope to acquire even more privileges, Westerners are waking up to the folly of having thrown open their borders to an alien civilization. At one time, Europeans understood from past experience what was at stake, as they protected themselves, for centuries, from further encroachment by Muslims, and their American cousins instinctively understood that there were limits to "assimilation."

But that was yesterday. Today, Muslims learned that, this time around, there was no need to attempt a siege of Paris with guns or swords. Instead, they are able to hold hostage entire streets in that city, while they perform their Friday prayers in public. It's a sort of in-your-face dare to the foolish Frenchman. The authorities must defer to this illegal activity, or risk the kind of chaos for which Muslims in France are already well known. Not only will there be no banning of the burka, there will be no imposition of unwanted rules, as Muslims let the French government know just who's boss.

"We have been in darkness for a long time," intoned Glenn Beck the night before his big rally. "We have been standing in spiritual darkness for decades." Yes, one could say that, but not for the reasons you cite, Mr. Beck.

[219]

Maybe that darkness will be lifted when Whites finally extricate themselves from decades of witless but safe obsessions like cheerleading for obscene wars, dancing to the demands of civil rights hustlers, acting as self-appointed watch-keepers over who is deemed a true "patriot," presuming to be able to read the mind and intentions of God, and intruding into the birthing predilections of strangers.

At some point these misguided conservatives must turn their attention away from delusions and focus on the explicit needs of their own race, instead of fearing to deal with the unspeakable—that is, diminishing as a group into minority numbers—60 percent, 40 percent, 20 percent. It will certainly mean stepping into a more dangerous zone (and Whites do like to play it safe), but there's not much time left to muster the courage, if they truly want to preserve (or, more accurately, *rescue*) the core of that which the Founders set out to establish.

If these Whites ever get their priorities straight, who knows what they might accomplish? Perhaps they might begin by ceasing to expend so much energy on admonishing others for opting not to have children and, instead, begin a crusade among their own people to raise the birth rates of Whites. Wouldn't it be remarkable if there were a reversal of what now appears to be the inevitable?

[220] Such an appeal to procreation could not be based on those ugly harangues about "sin" and "murder," in which conservatives love to indulge, but on a sense of pride and a concern for the future custodianship of this country. Of course, White reproductive rates might never be able to outstrip those of the Muslims and other Third Worlders, but a sound, restrictive immigration policy would go a long way towards evening up the demographics. If they fail to turn their focus to such realities, just who do these conservatives think are most likely to work at preserving the foundational institutions of the country they supposedly yearn to "take back?"

At his rally, Beck told over a quarter of a million hopeful Whites that the emergence of the Tea Parties and similar entities of discontented citizens is evidence of "the beginning of the Great Awakening in America." Would that were so. ❧

The

ANTI-CIVILIZATION

COLIN LIDDELL

Nothing is
at the heart of
the West.

COLIN LIDDELL
is a Tokyo-based journalist
and Contributing Editor at
Alternative Right.

[*images*]
"Horizon"
Los Angeles, California
Wikimedia

"McWorld"
Muscat, Oman
Wikimedia

In his famous book [225]

The Clash of Civilizations and the Remaking of World Order
(1996), Samuel P. Huntington put forward the thesis, popular
with large sections of the "Right," that the post-Cold-War world
would be shaped by its major civilizations and their interactions.[1]

For some, it was the gently coded recognition of race
that appealed; for others, it was the stigmatization of Islam as a
rather unpleasant civilization that rang true; whatever the case,
the book became, for better or worse, a landmark of political
science. This makes it an ideal starting point for considering the
topic of civilizations in general and the problematic nature of the
West in particular.

---

[1]   Samuel P. Huntington, *The Class of Civilizations and the Remaking of
      World Order* (New York: Simon & Schuster, 1996).

Clash is well written in that it deploys supportive data for its theories in the correct amounts and at reassuring intervals, but there is also an extremely misshapen feel to Huntington's thesis that stems from the following factors:

[1]   Overemphasis on religion

[2]   Questionable demarcation of civilizational boundaries

[3]   Superficial definition of civilization

[4]   Cowardice regarding race

[5]   Confusion about the true nature of the West

[226]

QUIBBLES

The map showing the "World of Civilizations" in Huntington's book presents nine civilizations, namely Western, Latin American, African, Islamic, Sinic (Chinese), Hindu (Indian), Orthodox (largely Russian), Buddhist, and Japanese.

Huntington's scheme relies heavily on religion as a defining factor. This is especially noticeable in his Buddhist "civilization," which includes such disparate countries and climate zones as Thailand, Tibet, and Mongolia—three countries that have little in common except for the fact that they are Buddhist. Given their relative unimportance, it would perhaps have been more elegant to have simply included them as peripheral regions of Sinic civilization.

Religion is also the unacknowledged basis for his Western civilization, which throws together Catholic and Protestant countries, while strangely excluding heavily Europeanized parts of South America and Africa. Given the widespread lack of faith in most of the West, this seems odd. Religion also allows him to divide Russia and its satellites from the West—with Greece thrown in as a kind of going away present. Another major problem is India. Just as American maps of the world have two Indias, one on each side, so Huntington seems to think there are two, allocating the whole country to both the Islamic and Hindu civilizations.

Huntington makes a strong case for the inherent aggressiveness of Islamic civilization, based on the number of intra-civilizational and inter-civilizational conflicts[2]. This is something that has given the book neoconservative appeal, but there are other obvious explanations for this aggression, like Islam's comparative lack of political unity and the fact that it borders more civilizations than other civilizations.

[227]

One of the weaknesses of Huntington's book is that he is never clear about what a civilization actually is. His best definition comes on page 43, but is sketchy and subjective:

> *A civilization is the broadest cultural entity. Villages, regions, ethnic groups, nationalities, religious groups, all have distinct cultures at different levels of cultural heterogeneity... A*

---

[2] *Ibid.*, 256-258.

civilization is thus the highest cultural grouping of people and the broadest level of cultural identity people have short of that which distinguishes humans from other species. . . . Civilizations are the biggest "we" within which we feel culturally at home as distinguished from all the other "thems" out there.

The key point in this definition is that a civilization is something that people "feel" comfortable belonging to. Rather than just being a member of the same civilization that your parents were part of, it is now far more important how you "feel" about it.

This effectively turns "civilization" into an expression of late 20th-century consumerism. Your civilization could almost be something you pick off the shelf, like a pack of soap powder. Needless to say, following this principle in practice would cause havoc with Huntington's civilizational map.

The reason Huntington favors religion as the civilizational "sorting hat" is that it loosely reflects race and therefore gives his thesis a quality readers can empathize with, but also allows him to avoid mentioning the dreaded R-word itself—quite literally, as the book's index has no mention of "race" or its equivalents!

The idea of distinct zonal civilizations, however, is implicitly racial because such civilizations can only emerge through a degree of sustained demographic stability. Left-wing critics of Huntington realize this and have concentrated their attacks on this point.

To talk about Western civilization as Huntington does, is to slyly evoke the idea of Western European man. Western civilization is how the phrase "White race" is whispered in the modern, politically correct era. Huntington must have known this—and that implicit racialiam would likely make his book provocative and successful—but he also knew that he could not make race explicit. As a successful academic and part of the establishment, he had to maintain deniability. His slyness was his cowardice.

THE UNIQUENESS OF THE WEST

But enough about quibbles! The book's main weakness lies at its very heart, in the idea that the West is just another civilization, and an old one at that, dating from around the time of Charlemagne, according to Huntington. [229]

Huntington often admits that the West is unique among civilizations, but he fails to proceed to the next logical step, i.e. considering whether the West is in fact something entirely different:

> *The West obviously differs from all other civilizations that have ever existed in that it has had an overwhelming impact on all other civilizations that have existed since 1500. It also inaugurated the process of modernization and industrialization that have become worldwide, and as a result societies in all other civilizations have been attempting to catch up with the West*

in wealth and modernity. Do these characters of the West, however, mean that its evolution and dynamics as a civilization are fundamentally different from the patterns that have prevailed in all other civilizations? The evidence of history and the judgments of the scholars of the comparative history of civilizations suggest otherwise. The development of the West to date has not deviated significantly from the evolutionary patterns common to civilizations throughout history.

When he says that the West differs from all other civilizations, he appears to mean in terms of its power, technology, and early industrialization. He is therefore only describing effects rather than providing causes. This approach allows the power of the West to chime with the implicit Whiteness evoked by his civilizational categories, giving his readers a quiet, sweaty-palmed moment of racial smugness. It becomes more and more apparent that the book is subliminal, low-key, middle-brow White Pride porn. But mental masturbation is just mental masturbation, an action by the impotent to feel potent. It does not help us to understand civilization or the problem posed by the West.

[230]

If the West is different from all other civilizations, then that is clearly important, but Huntington shows little inclination to explore this question, even though it cries out for deeper analysis. But just how are we to approach this? Standard academic procedure would be to select your preferred theory first and then sift through a welter of micro data until you found facts and figures that confirmed your pre-selected view.

Rather than following this disingenuous course, I will refer to macro empirical points of comparison that will establish the uniqueness of the West in an easily observed and objective way. My three areas of comparison are:

[1]   Civilizational Morphology

[2]   Civilizational Consistency

[3]   Civilizational Behavior

CIVILIZATIONAL MORPHOLOGY

Like countries, civilizations have definite shapes. Although their borders may be less precise, they tend to occupy specific parts of the globe. Using this as an empirical standard, we can see that all civilizations except the West have a reasonably compact form.

[231]

The West by contrast has a divided and disparate form: the core is in Europe, the largest piece is thousands of miles further West, and there are other pieces scattered all around the globe in such far flung places as Australia, New Zealand, and, according to Huntington's map, even French Guyana.

This patchy pattern would be even more apparent if the more European parts of South America and Africa were included in the West. But then, that would have raised the issue of race in too explicit a manner for Huntington's liking.

Interestingly, disparate morphology is something that can also be detected in the Medieval West, and in the main civilization that preceded the West, namely the Roman Empire.

With Western enclaves in Palestine, parts of Greece, the remoter regions of the Baltic, and even Greenland, as well as an alien civilization occupying much of the Iberian Peninsula, the Medieval West was also an oddly shaped civilization. The same could be said for the Roman Empire, whose main problem throughout its history was cumbersome, over-extended borders—for example, Dacia. In strict morphological terms, The West and its predecessors have always lacked the compactness common to almost all other civilizations. Imperial overstretch has always been with us.

[232]

CIVILIZATIONAL CONSISTENCY

Another major empirical point of difference between the West and all other civilizations is in civilizational consistency over time. The essence of a civilization should not radically alter over the centuries. A consistent core of features, customs, and qualities will normally be retained. China today is still recognizably the same civilization as China of the Ming or Han period. Similar points could be made regarding Islamic and Hindu civilizations, and even the intensely modernized Japanese civilization.

The West by contrast shows marked inconsistencies. The values and characteristics of today are unrecognizable from those of 100 years ago, which are themselves markedly different from those of 500 years ago or 1000 years ago, when Christ was being peddled to the Danes as some kind of warrior god. In short, the West is flux.

CIVLIZATIONAL BEHAVIOR

Due to people's limitations in geography and history, this is the most obvious difference between the West and the rest. There are things that normal civilizations do that the West simply doesn't do and *vice-versa*. We can break some of this down into the following categories:

[1]   Demography

[2]   Technology

[3]   Conflict

[4]   Propaganda

[233]

DEMOGRAPHY

Perhaps the most noticeable thing that the West doesn't do these days is defend itself demographically. The vast majority of civilizations, even in their dotages, attempt to prevent the demographic displacement of their peoples. the West, by contrast, is supposed to be the mightiest civilization, yet it freely allows and even assists widespread intrusion and colonization of its territories by outsiders.

Interestingly, the closest any other civilization has come to this is Islamic civilization, which has important macro-historical similarities with Christianity. This also encouraged large flows of people into its civilization in the form of slaves from the South and mercenaries from the North, accounting for some of the interesting genetic mixes to be found in the "Arab" countries, but even in this case, there was a clear attempt to keep the incomers subordinated, although in the case of the Seljuk and Mameluke 'slave mercenaries' this clearly backfired.

[234] The West by contrast offers its invaders free medical care, housing, welfare, and a host of other benefits, including a half share in the Presidency of the United States. Also, the more different the invaders are, the more it seems to welcome and assist them. While eastern Europeans are expected to work as the price of admission into western Europe, Somalians, Afghans, and Congolese merely have to show up. This effectively gives a green light for various forms of race replacement and the radical alteration of the demographic character of the civilization.

Considering all previously existing civilizations, these patterns of behavior are simply an aberration. Some try to pass this off as an effect of modernity, but even civilizations that are as modern and economically developed as the West, like Japanese civilization and parts of the Sinic civilization, refuse to behave like this.

TECHNOLOGY

Another behavior pattern of the West is equally unique and baffling. While all civilizations try jealously to guard their business, military, and technological advantages, the West goes out of its way to facilitate massive transfers of technology and manufacturing capability.

The Chinese famously carefully guarded their economic secrets, banning the export of silk worms and tea plants so that these had to be smuggled out of the country; while the secrets of porcelain production were so carefully guarded that they had to be independently reinvented by the potters of Meissen.

[235]

CONFLICT

All civilizations will enter into conflict with other civilizations for a range of understandable if not always commendable reasons. Sometimes these conflicts have played a vital role in human progress. the West, however, is unique for the pointlessness of its conflicts. This is especially true today, where we are being treated to TV images of squaddies doing the rounds in Afghan villages while non-profit organizations try to translate *The Female Eunuch* into Farsi.

Again, there is a temptation to see this as some kind of side effect of modernity, but it is also possible to find Medieval and Classical examples that bear a surprising resemblance, most notably in the Crusades and Roman attempts to subjugate economically unimportant wildernesses, such as Germania and Caledonia. Before this, there were also the heroic but essentially pointless campaigns of Alexander the Great in Central Asia.

PROPAGANDA

Normal civilizations have identity. Those who belong to them know, without thinking or conscious statement, exactly who they are. They exude what they are rather than proclaim it. the West, by contrast, is always trying to publicize and propagandize what it is, repeatedly affirming and broadcasting its values, as if not quite sure of them. The reason for this is quite simple. The values of the West are for the most part meaningless universalisms and negatives that can only exist in a state of constant affirmation.

THE VALUES OF THE WEST

Before I precisely explain the negativity of these values, it is useful to establish context by examining how the characteristics of Western civilization have changed.

Huntington's definition of the characteristics is a bit of a grab bag along the lines of "what those other guys said," but the format of the middle-brow academic book forces him to bullet point his confusion. He lists the following as the defining characteristics of the West before it modernized:

[1]   The Classical legacy

[2]   Catholicism and Protestantism

[3]   European languages

[4]   Separation of spiritual and temporal authority

[5]   Social pluralism (also described as the existence of "diverse autonomous groups")

[6]   Representative bodies (by which he means multi-polar parliaments, such as the French Estates or the British Houses of Lords and Commons)

[237]

[7]   Individualism

It is noticeable that rather than defining the West as it exists today, he is forced to rewind by 200 or 300 years, and even then, he admits that many of the elements listed above were not exclusive to the West. But this is the closest that he comes to defining Western Civilization, so we should be grateful for that at least.

An examination of these seven characteristics of the West immediately drives home the major empirical point about the *civilizational inconsistency* of the West. What Huntington is describing is demonstrably not the West in which we live. The past in this case is not so much another country as another civilization.

Viewed from the present, this list starts to fall apart and mutate in front of our eyes. Points (1), (2), (4), and (6) have clearly not dated well. Also, even in an earlier historical era, (4) effectively counteracted and minimized the influence of (2), which is very much the case today, where religion is largely relegated to a personal issue of less social importance than one's hairstyle.

If we attempt to maintain the principle of civilizational consistency by staying as close to Huntington's list as possible, we still have to make significant changes to update it for our own times.

[238]

We would have to discard (1) and (4) entirely. The Classical legacy is now confined to the extremely unfashionable end of academia, while the separation of spiritual and temporal authority only makes sense in a society that has a strong spiritual authority, which is clearly not the case with the West. Of the five remaining points, (2), (3), (5), and (6) would have to be radically redefined.

Catholicism and Protestantism would shrink to become "minor identitarian role for Christianity (optional);" European languages would have to be altered to reflect the increasing linguistic diversity of the West, perhaps substituting the term

"Tower of Babel;" the "diverse autonomous groups" of the social pluralism category could be replaced with "diverse racial and sexual identity groups"; and Representative bodies could be altered to "Pooled electorate with detached professional political class." The two defunct characteristics could be replaced by two new characteristics. As the Classical legacy was mainly enshrined in our universities, this gap could be filled with "cultural Marxism and political correctness," which holds sway there now; while the element of denial implicit in the old separation of spiritual and temporal authority could be served by replacing it with anti-nationalism, which might also be termed "White guilt." This would give us the following heavily revised Huntingtonian list of characteristics to define the West as we now know it:

[239]

[1]   Cultural Marxism and political correctness

[2]   Minor identitarian role for Christianity (optional)

[3]   Tower of Babel

[4]   White Guilt

[5]   Social pluralism (diverse racial and sexual identity groups)

[6]   Pooled electorate and detached professional political class

[7]   Individualism

CIVILIZATION IS POSITIVE

While this is amusing, trying to stick with Huntington's categories is obviously akin to taking the long way round. When people talk about "Western values" today, they invariably mean things like "freedom," "choice," "individualism," "equality," "human rights," etc. These are lovely words and, indeed, words that most of us instinctively agree on. But the reason we love these words is because of their negativity and vacuity.

"Negative" is a loaded word, so I am forced here to "unload" it. By negative I don't mean bad, bleak, or depressing, but negative in the almost mathematical sense of something missing—a gap, a space, that which is unfilled and unformed, a void.

This is why we like these words. It is their very vacuity that draws us in. When we hear these terms we instantly think of our own freedom, our own choice, and our own individual natures. In other words, we take a hollow word and fill it with ourselves. "Freedom" in itself is meaningless. It only becomes meaningful when we imagine how we would use it. This explains the power and popularity of such rhetoric. But when the principle is extended throughout a whole society or civilization, then problems are sure to arise.

While we crave our freedom, we may object to that of others. The heterosexual may scorn the openly homosexual (and *vice versa*), the indigenous may resent the assertive incomer (and *vice versa*), so that "freedom," "choice," "individualism," and the rest of them have to be enforced from above, creating a tendency towards totalitarianism that goes hand in hand with the apparently affirmative individualism of these negative values.

True civilization, by its very nature, is collective and positive, and as a result does not require the statist imposition of "values." It seeks to create a degree of similarity and sympathy between people through shared culture, history, morality, and habits. This can only be done through "positive" values.

But, once again, "positive" is a loaded word, so I will have to "unload" that, too. By positive I don't mean good, fine, or dandy, but positive in the almost mathematical sense of something that is *there*, something clear and substantial, a decided idea, a belief, a definite opinion, not a mental vacuum.

[241]

One of the functions of civilization is to shape its people, to give them a collective set of precepts, a way of looking at the world, and an identity. The West, by contrast, is based on the negation of this civilizational idea. Any residue of this, such as Christian notions that homosexuality is wrong or sentimentality about national identity, are attacked by the establishment and the controlled culture of the "Anti-civilization."

By destroying the collective and corrective principles of civilization, the West that we see today threatens its own unity and is therefore forced to rely on totalitarian substitutes.

The morality of the West becomes the enforcement of the anti-morality: gay rights, the mass murder of fetuses, a culture of divorce and one-parent families, the privileges of the immigrant over the rights of the indigenous, the enforced equivalence of all forms of dysfunction with normalcy; while its identitarianism becomes a negative one of not belonging to the despised groups, the "racists," "neo-Nazis," and "haters," who crave a positive civilizational identity.

THE "NATURAL CIVILIZATION"

But where did something as unique and frightening as the Anti-civilization come from? It is not simply the product of a few decades of Leftist agitation, nor is it down to a cadre of sneaky Ashkenazi. The roots of the problem predate the influence of those two often interrelated groups by at least two millennia.

The rootless Anti-civilization has deep roots that pass through and play their part in much that could be counted civilization. But in order to diagnose disease, you first need to define health. In order to do this, we need a working idea of a "natural civilization."

Luckily I happen to live in a reasonable approximation to one. Of the nine civilizations that Huntington includes in his book, the smallest is Japan, my home for the last several years. So, what characteristics would we associate with the "natural civilization"? Simple deductive reasoning suggests the following:

[1]   Geographical identity

[2]   Cultural continuity

[3]   Demographic continuity

[4]   Centricity (symbolic, cultural, or religious centers and heartlands)

[5]   Local rootedness

[6]   Modulated openness

(These characteristics are related to the macro-empirical points used to establish the uniqueness of the West, namely, morphology, consistency, and behavior.)

[243]

Japanese civilization is strong in all six of the above characteristics. Being an archipelago, it has a clear geographical identity and it has existed continuously for thousands of years. This has allowed it to develop a high degree of centricity, through cultural and religious centres like Kyoto and Ise, and local rootedness, with people feeling deeply attached to their hometowns and the graves of ancestors.

A possible drawback with the first four factors is civilizational parochialism, which can be impoverishing in terms of technology and other ideas. However, Japan has always been open to other cultures and civilizations, mainly the Sinic and Western civilizations, and it has been able to enrich its civilization without destroying it or seeing it replaced.

Left to themselves, most civilizations have a tendency to develop along similar lines, although clearly each would do so in its own way, at its own level, and relative to its environment and the qualities of its people. A similar pattern can be seen in the Sinic and Hindu civilizations, as well as several that are no longer with us, such as the Andean and Meso-American.

GESTATION OF THE ANTI-CIVILIZATION

With the idea of the "natural civilization" to guide us, we can now detect anomalies in the development of the Anti-civilization of the West that will help us to understand its aberrant nature. There are three main historical stages in the creation of the Anti-civilization, each of which was also partly a reaction to its predecessor:

[244]

[1]   Romanization

[2]   Christianization

[3]   Liberalization

What is known as the *Alternative Right* includes several tendencies, including neo-paganism and neo-Christianity. The latter see the evils of the modern West as springing from secularization, while the former see Christianity as the root of the problem. Both groups clearly perceive part of the bigger picture.

ROMANIZATION

While the growth of Sinic civilization was broadly based on a large ethnic Han population, the growth of the Roman Empire at roughly the same time was not. This was the result of differential demographic and geographic factors, with the Romans starting from a smaller population base and expanding across a more disjointed land mass.

Unlike the main population centers of Europe and the Mediterranean, which are divided into peninsulas and islands, or by the sea or the Alps, the centre of Chinese population is united by the surrounding mountains, desert, and sea. This favored geographical identity, demographic and cultural continuity, centricity, and local rootedness. Roman civilization, by contrast, became more decentered as it grew, developing, via conquest, military occupation, demilitarization of the conquered, and an uprooted slave population. Power moved increasingly to the periphery, as that was where the army was located.

[245]

As the Roman Empire weakened politically, economically, and militarily, its natural geographical and ethnic disunity reasserted itself. Parts of the Empire reverted to older ethnic cultures—Greeks and Berbers, for example—but in much of the empire, a demographic void had been created into which new peoples (mainly Germans and later in the East, Arabs) were drawn. Contrast this with the Sinic or Hinducivilizations. Even when the dynasties collapsed, demographic stability remained.

CHRISTIANIZATION

The processes of Romanization and Christianization overlap. (Islamification, which occurred in the eastern and southern part of the Roman Empire at a later date, is a related phenomenon that reflects similar forces.)

As a civilization struggling with its geographical ambiguity, demographic divisions, lack of rootedness, and fluctuating centricity, Roman civilization was drawn to Christianity because of its transcendent, reductionist and centralizing qualities. The emperors saw it as a means of tightening their grip on society as the Empire built around that society waned. In other words, it served as a substitute for the organic unity that the Empire lacked.

[246]

With the Empire sliding further into chaos, Christianity then effectively became the shadow Empire. Unable to better the barbarian hordes in battle, the civilization retreated into its churches and monasteries and set about rebuilding its power through offering the barbarian rulers the same advantages that it offered the Emperors.

By making its power less ostensible, Christianity was also able to spread much further than Rome's legions had. Along with the remnants of Roman civilization and the Germanic cultures of the dominant invaders, it also provided the basis for a new civilization, which Huntington calls

Western. Given the problems of civilizational consistency, it would be more accurate to see this as a predecessor of the West, called Christian civilization, which lasted at least into the late 18th century.

Just as the characteristics of Roman civilization—militarism, imperialism, colonization, Romanization, and a rootless slave population—derived from the degree to which that civilization deviated from the conditions of the "natural civilization," so, too, with Christian civilization, which also lacked geographic and demographic contiguity, centricity, and rootedness.

A vast disparate geographical area, containing a wide variety of people, was united by this civilization. As its power spread and tightened, its unnaturalness became increasingly manifest in the following symptoms:

[247]

[1]   Brainwashed rootless elite

[2]   Geographical incontinence

[3]   The repression of localism

[4]   Cultural schizophrenia

[5]   Outbreaks of mass hysteria

The Church decultured and denatured its recruits, removing them from their original culture, and even from their roles as men and warriors or women and mothers. Christian civilization had no geographical sense of itself. This was manifest in its frequent attempts to missionarize and convert distant lands as well as in the Crusades. In short, it was geographically incontinent.

Partly this was the result of its rootless and otherworldly nature. As a corollary of this, it also strongly repressed any traces of localism, destroying local gods and traditions or subsuming them into its own pantheon of saints and calendar of festivals.

The fact that it could not subjugate directly as the Romans had done, also meant that Christian civilization developed into a schizophrenic culture, with religious and secular sides. The secular side tended to develop in the direction of the "natural civilization," leading to the creation of the German Reich, while the religious side tended to oppose this.

[248]

The unnaturalness of these various arrangements led to constant strains as well as an element of paranoia resulting in increasing hysteria that was reflected in purges of heretics, crusades, inquisitions, Antipopes, and finally schisms and sectarianism. The fanaticism expressed in these acts is testament to the *unnaturalness* of this civilization.

While the modern West can be defined by its "negative" values, Christian civilization was defined by an excess of "positive" values, imperatives designed to shape and control every aspect of life from diet, dress, and belief to art, music, and architecture. This was all part of its unnatural attempt to impose an order and unity that was not naturally there.

Islamic civilization in the southern and eastern Mediterranean, Persia, and Central Asia, represents a similar drive to impose artificial civilizational unity on an unwieldy and diverse area.

LIBERALIZATION

Civilizations that approximate more to the conditions of the "natural civilization," such as the Hindu, Sinic, and Japanese civilizations, seldom feel the need to be as imperative as either the Christian or Islamic civilizations. The process by which they shape their populations is less overt but more immersive.

[249]

Between the fall of the old Christian civilization, which can be linked for the sake of convenience to the date of the French Revolution, and the rise of the Anti-civilization of the West, which we can peg to the 1960s, there was an intermediate period of nearly 200 years, during which Christianity remained important, especially as a force for social cohesion, but was increasingly subordinated to a secular, materialist culture, economy, and ruling elite. It seems natural to refer to this intervening entity as secular Christian civilization.

FROM POSITIVE TO NEGATIVE

The exact processes by which Christian civilization led to secular Christian civilization, and then the modern West, are extremely complex, but a review of the main macro empirical factors correlated with the concept of a "natural civilization" suggest that the West and its predecessors—the Roman, Christian, and secular Christian civilizations—occupy a vector of civilizational instability that works against the conditions of the ideal "natural civilization."

This instability, which is partly geographical in origin, generates civilizations with extreme characteristics that emerge as reactions to their predecessors, in a kind of wild zigzagging pattern: the overly aggressive militarism of the Romans is succeeded by the passive aggression and positivist morality of the Christians, which is then supplanted by the negative idealism and totalitarian tendencies of the modern West.

The latest stage of this process has created a civilization that can best be described as an Anti-civilization, as it is founded on what are essentially "negative" values rather than the "positive" ones that characterize all other and preceding civilizations.

There is a tendency on the Right to view the characteristics of the modern West as symptoms of long-term decline and to conclude, along with Huntington, that what we are witnessing is the Spenglerian sunset of an aged civilization. But the modern West as a distinct—and it is very distinct—entity is at most only a mere four decades old.

So, how will this new Anti-civilization of the West play out? As a new geopolitical mutation, is it inherently unstable and liable to collapse within decades (rather than centuries), or will it achieve a stable symbiosis with the global economy? Also, will its anti-values, with their strong subjective appeal, contaminate and corrode the other civilizations, creating a soulless and necessarily totalitarian global system? And what of the fate of those already living under its baleful influence, the largest part the White European race? Will they find a way to reject and overthrow the Anti-civilization from within, or will they continue to unwittingly support it as it inexorably grinds them down into minority status? This raises one last question, is the Anti-civilization dependent for its existence on the dominance of this race, and with its fall, will it also see its own end?   ❧   [251]

The

ROOTS

of the

WHITE MAN

SAMUEL FRANCIS

*Is Occidental culture
doomed to embrace
tolerance, democracy,
and minority rights?
Or are such dictums
perversions of a
lost Aryan ideal?*

SAMUEL T. FRANCIS (1947-2005)

originally published "The Roots of the White Man" in *American Renaissance* in the fall of 1996. He chose to write the article under the pseudonym "Edwin Clark." Editor Jared Taylor suggests that this was due to the fact that Francis was treading into scholarly matters outside his specialty of English History.

"Roots" was written as a response to an earlier essay by Taylor, but with the passage of time, it has come to stand on its own as Francis's definitive statement on the distinctive, fundamental characteristics of Occidental civilization and the White race. Taylor had argued that much of White people's racially destructive behaviour, such as inviting non-Whites into their societies and giving them advantages over their offspring—as well as other altruistic behavior, such as support for the welfare of animals— derive from a deep, innate preference for "fairness." Though not entirely disagreeing with Taylor, Francis sought to rediscover the West as a Faustian, imperial culture—one whose distinctive primal drives are towards discovery and domination, not "equal rights."

[254]

Samuel Francis was one of the most literate and compelling writers to have made a living as a political pundit and Washington, DC, operative. His career also stands as a testament to the power of political correctness and the cowardliness of the self-styled "conservative movement." With a doctorate from the University of North Carolina and experience as a senatorial advisor, Francis had established himself as an arch-conservative columnist at the rightward-leaning *Washington Times*. But his willingness to discuss, quite frankly, racial hypocrisy and guilt-mongering—and, more provocative, White identity and pride—unmade his career. He quickly went from insider to outsider and, anticipating subsequent conservative cleansings, he became unmentionable for his erstwhile colleagues.

In the end, Francis's purging proved to be a liberation, as he moved beyond Republican politics as a writer, editor, and organizer. One such endeavour was his co-founding of the publishing house responsible for this journal. In 2005, at a point when his second career was reaching its culmination, Francis died of an aneurysm at the age of 57.

~**Richard B. Spencer**

[*image*]
"Under Wraps"
Nina Kouprianova (2012)

By looking at the deep racial-cultural history of whites since ancient times, we discover more profoundly who we are, where we come from, and where we may be going. We may also learn how to control those traits that are now contributing to our destruction and to make use of them and other, more fundamental ones that can help place us back on the path toward what should be our racial destiny.

When speaking of "whites," I mean the branch of the Caucasian race now generally called "Indo-Europeans," or what used to be known as "Aryans," whose descendants today constitute the main part of the populations of Europe, North America, Australia, and New Zealand. The term "Aryan" has, for obvious reasons, gone out of fashion, but prior to the rise of German National Socialism, it was a widely accepted anthropological label, and the great archaeologist V. Gordon Childe wrote a book entitled *The Aryans* (1926), which remains a useful survey of what was then known of the origins and early history of the ancestors of European man.

Whether we employ the term "Aryan" or "Indo-European," however, most anthropologists today use these terms merely as linguistic or at most cultural labels and insist that they do not refer to race. Yet this usage seems artificial. The early Indo-Europeans, no matter where they lived or where their remains have been found, were white, and their physical remains, art, and languages reflect their essential racial unity, regardless of the diversity of the subracial stocks into which they eventually divided in various parts of the world and the mixtures with other stocks and races that eventually absorbed many of them.

[256]

The Indo-Europeans are thought to have originated in the steppes of Russia and began to move out of that area into what is now eastern and northern Europe, the Near East, and India in the third or second millennium B.C. The earliest known written Indo-European language is the Linear B script of the Greek city-state of Mycenae around 1500 B.C., and it was around this time also that the Aryans invaded India and displaced the dying Dravidian civilizations of the Indus Valley.

In Europe, the Aryan invaders conquered and displaced the non-Indo-European peoples of the archaic megalithic civilization that built Stonehenge and similar colossal monuments. In the Near East and India, the Indo-

Europeans conquered many peoples who had created literate, urban civilizations. In some cases, the Aryans were, to a greater or lesser degree, absorbed into the larger populations they had conquered.

Of particular interest to us are the common features of archaic Indo-European peoples, which continue to shape modern Indo-European-derived beliefs and institutions. As the French folklorist Georges Dumézil has pointed out, one of the principal characteristics of early Indo-European societies is a hierarchical, three-tiered or "tripartite" class structure of priests, warriors, and herder-cultivators. This structure appears to be racially rooted and prefigures many of the societal characteristics we now think of as typically Western or European. [257]

The Indo-Europeanist J.P. Mallory has pointed out one of the central elements of this Indo-European three-class society:

> [O]ne of the more obvious symbols of social tripartition is colour, emphasized by the fact that both ancient India and Iran expressed the concept of caste with the word for colour (varna). A survey of the social significance of different colours is fairly clear cut, at least for the first two functions. Indo-Iranian, Hittite, Celtic and Latin ritual all assign white to priests and red to the warrior. The third would appear to have been marked by a darker colour such as black or blue.[1]

---

[1] J.P. Mallory, *In Search of the Indo-Europeans: Language, Archaeology and Myth* (London: Thames and Hudson, 1989), 133.

The racial symbolism of such caste colors is obvious, with the higher ranks of society being symbolized by the color associated with the lighter-skinned Aryans and the lower ranks symbolized by the darker hues of the conquered non-Aryan races.

Indeed, racial consciousness among the early Aryans was commonplace. Romila Thapar, a modern Indian scholar, writes,

> *The first step in the direction of caste (as distinct from class) was taken when the Aryans treated the Dasas [non-Aryans] as beyond the social pale, probably owing to a fear of the Dasas and the even greater fear that assimilation with them would lead to a loss of Aryan identity. Ostensibly the distinction was largely that of colour, the Dasas being darker and of an alien culture. . . . The colour-element of caste was emphasized, throughout this period, and was eventually to become deep-rooted in north-Indian Aryan culture. Initially, therefore, the division was between the Aryans and the non-Aryans.*[2]

[258]

The Laws of Manu, the ancient Sanskrit code of social obligations for Hinduism, is very explicit about the consequences of interracial marriage:

> *An unknown man, of no (visible) class but born of a defiled womb and no Aryan, may seem to have the form of an Aryan, but he can be discovered by his own innate activities. Un-Aryan behaviour, harshness, cruelty, and habitual failure to perform*

---

[2] Romila Thapar, *A History of India* (Baltimore, Md.: Penguin Books, 1966), 37-38.

> *the rituals are the manifestations in this world*
> *indicating that a man is born of a defiled womb....*
> *But the kingdom in which these degraded bastards*
> *are born, defiling the classes, quickly perishes,*
> *together with the people who live there.*[3]

Whatever modern scholars may say about the old Aryans being merely a language group and not a race, that does not seem to be the way the old Aryans themselves looked upon the question.

Dumézil's "tripartition thesis" shows that the archaic Indo-Europeans throughout the world possessed a remarkably similar social structure and common culture extending well beyond language and including the ordering of society and religion. One of Dumézil's leading students, C. Scott Littleton, points out a crucial way in which Indo-European societies differed from those of non-Indo-Europeans.

[259]

> *The food-producing class, while distinct from that of*
> *the warriors, was nevertheless a much more integral*
> *part of the total society.... The ancient I-E [Indo-*
> *European] herdsmen and cultivators—and perhaps*
> *the artisans as well—would seem to have played a part*
> *in the total ritual and social life of their communities*
> *undreamed of by the ancestors of the Egyptian*
> *fellahin and their counterparts in Mesopotamia.*[4]

---

[3]   *The Laws of Manu*, Ed. and Trans. Wendy Doniger (New York: Penguin Books, 1991), 10: 57-61

[4]   C. Scott Littleton, *The New Comparative Mythology: An Anthropological Assessment of the Theories of Georges Dumézil* (rev. ed., Los Angeles: University of California Press, 1973), 224.

The subordinate but distinct social and political role for the "third class" ensured a level of participation in the community unknown to the wholly dominated peasants of the Asiatic non-Aryan peoples. This may help account for the eventual appearance of participatory and representative (republican and democratic) political systems among the Aryan peoples.

Moreover, the separation of the military and religious functions into distinct classes points to an early Indo-European tendency toward a distinction between the sacred and the secular that seems to be entirely unique to the Indo-European peoples and which may be the foundation of the later differentiation of science and philosophy from religion in European society, as well [260] as the source of the conflict between secular and ecclesiastical authority in European history.

Finally, this ordering of society and social function was conceived as having supernatural or cosmic sanction and was held to be in accord with the order of nature. Some scholars believe that the tripartite structure of Indo-European society survived into Medieval Europe with the division of society into "those who work, those who fight, and those who pray," and it may also be reflected in the division of political functions into executive, judicial, and legislative in the U.S. Constitution, and even in the Christian idea of the Trinity.

It is possible to extract from the mythology of the Aryans and from the remains of their cultures and literature certain more abstract concepts that seem to be common to most or all Aryan societies and continue to characterize those of their descendants. Perhaps in unconscious accord with the quaint Aryan custom of tripartition, I will try to identify three such traits and to elaborate on their significance.

COSMIC ORDER

It is a widespread feature of early Aryan thought that there exists an objective order that is independent of what we believe or want to believe—in other words, truth. The *Rig Veda* calls this order *rta*, a term that may be linked with the word Arya itself, which seems to mean "noble" in *The Laws of Manu.* [261] The word "Aryan" comes from "Arya" and a number of other Indo-European words seem to be connected—the Greek *arete* (virtue, the quality of acting like a man, from which we derive "aristocracy"); the Latin *ara* (altar) and the name "Arthur." But regardless of the linguistic linkages, the Aryan concept of Cosmic Order contrasts with ideas of the universe found among ancient non-Aryans. For the latter, Cosmic Order is merely the product of will, a creature of magic, and it can change if those who know how to change it wish to do so. If the priests or the divine king did not perform the proper magical rituals, the sun literally would not rise, the Nile would not flood, and food would not grow. In this non-Aryan, magical view of nature, order does not exist as an externally independent and objective arrangement of nature and its functioning.

While early Aryans did believe in and practice magic, theirs was not a world-view in which nature and the universe were dependent on magic. Magic could be used to influence nature (through love potions or ointments to make weapons stronger and the like), but nature itself exists apart from the tricks of the magicians and sorcerers. Indeed, throughout Western history, magicians and sorcerers almost always come from pre-Aryan Mother Goddess figures or from the non-Aryan Orient— from Egypt, Babylonia, or the "Magi" of pre-Aryan Persia, from whom we get the word "magic."

Moreover, Indo-European gods are considerably less powerful than the deities adored by the non-Aryans. Zeus, Apollo, Odin, Thor, and the rest did not create the universe and are in fact subject to most of its rules. The subordination of Aryan gods to the regularities of the universe itself points toward a deep Indo-European belief in Cosmic Order, a belief that has major philosophical and ethical implications.

[262]

It follows from recognition of the Cosmic Order that some things are true and some aren't, no matter what you prefer to think, that some things will always be and always have been true or false, regardless of your wishes, and that some things will happen or will not happen, whether you like it or not. Hence the Greek and Nordic ideas of "Fate" or "Destiny," that some things are beyond the control of the human will and are inevitable because of the very fabric of the universe. The concept of Fate is probably the origin of the principle of causality and the ancestor of such Indo-European ideas as logic, mathematics, philosophy, science, and theology.

While Egyptians and Babylonians collected a great deal of information about mathematics and astronomy and practiced impressive engineering on a grand scale, their "sciences" never had a really scientific basis. Their knowledge existed either as the lore collected by the priests or as the products of practical trial and error. Only the Indo-European Greeks actually systematized scientific and mathematical knowledge, and they were able to construct it into a system because the system itself was their concept of a Cosmic Order in which all events and phenomena were related through causality and its inexorable linkages of one event and phenomenon to another.

It is notable that Christian theology itself, as developed under the Scholastic theologians of the Middle Ages and under the influence of rationalistic Greek philosophy, reflects this underlying Indo-European belief, that even God behaves according to certain principles, just as Zeus and Odin did, and it is also interesting that today even Christian fundamentalists who wish to disprove the theory of evolution in behalf of their religious beliefs try to do so through "creation science." Among Indo-Europeans, even religion and the supernatural are subordinate to the ancient Aryan perception of a Cosmic Order that governs the universe from the remotest galaxies to the life-cycles of insects.

[263]

It is no accident," wrote V. Gordon Childe,

> *that the first great advances towards abstract natural science were made by the Aryan Greeks*

and the Hindus, not by the Babylonians or the Egyptians, despite their great material resources and their surprising progress in techniques—in astronomical observation for example. In the moralization of religion too Aryans have played a prominent role. The first great world religions which addressed their appeal to all men irrespective of race or nationality, Buddhism and Zoroastrianism, were the works of Aryans, propagated in Aryan speech. . . . It is certain that the great concept of the Divine Law or Cosmic Order is associated with the first Aryan peoples who emerge upon the stage of history some 3,500 years ago.[5]

[264]   It is from the Aryan concept of a Cosmic Order that modern white men derive their mental inclinations both to *universalism*, a tendency to think in terms of generalizations and abstractions that apply universally rather than in terms of the specific, local, and temporary, and to *objectivity*, the tendency to evaluate events and phenomena with reference to the general and the abstract, rather than to judge them subjectively, as they relate to themselves. While these traits account for many of the achievements of European man, they also, as we shall see, help to explain many of his racial problems in more recent times.

ETHICAL IMPLICATIONS

The concept of the Cosmic Order also has important ethical implications, and it was as an ethical system that the

[5]   V. Gordon Childe, *The Aryans: A Study of Indo-European Origins* (1926; reprinted., New York: Dorset Press, 1987), 4-5.

ancient Aryans mainly seem to have understood it. Recognition of a Cosmic Order implies that human action has consequences—that you cannot do whatever you please and expect nothing to come of it—and also that sometimes no matter what you do, you will not be able to avoid the consequences of your Fate, what the Greeks and Norsemen respectively called your *moira* or *wyrd*. Thus, the central concept of Greek tragedy is that the tragic hero suffers as a consequence of a "tragic flaw" that may not be the result of his will or intent but that makes his fate unavoidable. Oedipus was doomed to commit the sacrileges of patricide and incest through his very virtue, and there are many heroes in Greek mythology who encounter similar fates.

The ethical implication that Indo-Europeans drew from this belief is not that man should surrender or fecklessly seek to avoid his fate but rather that he should accept it courageously. Achilles in *The Iliad* knows that he is fated to die young but, as horrid as death is to Achilles, he readily prefers the glory of his brief heroic life to the obscurity of a long and safe existence. By contrast Gilgamesh, in the Mesopotamian epic, seeks only to avoid death and resorts to all sorts of magic and sorcery to prevent it.

[265]

In her survey of Norse myth, H.R. Ellis Davidson notes similar connections between fate, Cosmic Order, and the heroism of both gods and men:

> *In spite of this awareness of fate, indeed perhaps because of it, the picture of man's qualities which emerges from the myths is a noble one. The gods are heroic figures, men writ large, who led dangerous, individualistic lives, yet at the same time were*

part of a closely-knit small group, with a firm sense of values and certain intense loyalties. They would give up their lives rather than surrender these values, but they would fight on as long as they could, since life was well worthwhile. Men knew that the gods whom they served could not give them freedom from danger and calamity, and they did not demand that they should. We find in the myths no sense of bitterness at the harshness and unfairness of life, but rather a spirit of heroic resignation: humanity is born to trouble, but courage, adventure, and the wonders of life are matters of thankfulness, to be enjoyed while life is still granted to us. The great gifts of the gods were readiness to face the world as it was, the luck that sustains men in tight places, and the opportunity to win that glory which alone can outlive death.[6]

[266]

The Norse gods know that their race and the world are doomed at the final battle of Ragnarok, but they go out to fight and to meet their fate regardless. The concept of the "Last Stand," in which an outnumbered army of Aryan warriors faces battle against overwhelming odds, usually without any realistic expectation of victory, recurs throughout Indo-European history and legend—at the battles of Marathon and Thermopylae, Horatius at the Bridge, in the *Song of Roland*, in the Arthurian legends, at Ragnarok itself, or in the fiery climax of *Njal's Saga*, and at the Alamo, Rorke's Drift, and the Little Big Horn.

---

[6] H.R. Ellis Davidson, *Gods and Myths of Northern Europe* (Harmondsworth: Penguin Books, 1964), 218.

Indeed, Indo-European scholars have recognized a distinctive Indo-European myth pattern called the "Final Battle." As J.P. Mallory writes, "The epic traditions of a number of Indo-European peoples preserve an account of the 'final battle,' for example, Kurukshetra in the great Indian epic, the *Mahabharata*; the 'Second Battle of Mag Tured' among the early Irish; Ragnarok among the Norse; and several others."[7]

Moreover, the Indo-European hero, fighting in single combat, often is killed by treachery or trickery concocted by a non-Aryan or un-Aryan "trickster" figure. Thus, Achilles is killed by an arrow shot by the Trojan Paris, Hercules is killed by the trickery of a centaur, Theseus is pushed over a cliff from behind, Baldur is killed by the jealous trickery of Loki, Siegfried is killed by the treachery of his own brother-in-law, et cetera. It is interesting that in the biblical story of David and Goliath, the latter, a champion of the Aryan Philistines, is killed by the slingshot of David, and in the non-Aryan version recounted in the Old Testament, David's conduct is portrayed as an act of prowess.

[267]

The Aryan concept of Cosmic Order is thus closely linked to the scientific and philosophical achievements of Indo-European man as well as with his ethical ideas, especially with regard to Indo-European military behavior. The concept of Cosmic Order implied an essentially aristocratic obligation to carry out one's duty regardless of the consequences but also a heroic recognition of what the consequences, including death

[7]   Mallory, *In Search of the Indo-Europeans*, 129-30.

and destruction, might be. While other races and cultures have certainly displayed and idealized courage, heroism, and struggle against odds, none has incorporated these ideals into its fundamental world-view and ethic as fully as Indo-European man.

To say that belief in an external and objective cosmic order, independent of the human will and human action, is characteristic of the Aryan peoples is not to say that such an order actually exists, but rather that the Indo-European mind seems to be structured in such a way (perhaps due to neurological structures and processes peculiar to it), that it naturally thinks in terms of such an order and finds the world incomprehensible without it. In the absence of such a concept, we would be unable to make sense of the phenomena that we perceive; confronted by the mysteries of nature, life, and death, early Aryans sought to understand them by explaining them in terms of mythologies that reflected an underlying belief in a cosmic order and the duties it imposes on mortal men.

[268]

ARYAN DYNAMISM

Faustian dynamism is the quality that Oswald Spengler described as the unique trait of what he called the "Western Culture," characterized by the "Faustian soul, whose prime-symbol is pure and limitless space, and whose 'body' is the Western Culture."[8] In a general sense, Spengler is referring to the

---

[8] Oswald Spengler, *The Decline of the West* (2 vols.; trans. Charles Francis Atkinson; New York: Alfred A. Knopf, 1926), vol. 1, 183.

innovative, aggressive, creative, mobile, aspiring, inventive, and daring qualities that have always characterized Indo-Europeans.

Spengler also sharply distinguished the Western Faustian Culture from the "Apollinian" and "Magian" Cultures of the Classical Age and the Near East; but in fact, in the broader sense in which we are using the term here, the Greeks and Romans were also Faustian, and the Greek myth of Prometheus, the Titan who defied Zeus by giving mankind the gift of fire and was condemned to eternal torture because of his disobedience, is as much a Faustian myth as the Germanic legend of Faust himself, who dared to bargain with the Devil to gain knowledge and power and lost his soul because of his bargain.

[269]

Many Greek heroes exhibit similar traits of daring and eventually come to grief because of them, and these myths functioned not only as expressions of the Faustian tendencies of the Aryan people to push against limits and transgress established boundaries but also as cautionary tales that tried to warn men of the consequences of carrying their natural proclivities too far. While there is a superficial resemblance between these myths and the Hebraic story of Adam and Eve, there is also a significant difference. While Indo-European heroes often meet their doom because of or despite their heroism, Adam and Eve get kicked out of Eden merely because they disobeyed Yahweh. Neither one did anything particularly admirable or heroic, in contrast to Prometheus, Achilles, Hercules, Theseus, and many other Greek and Aryan heroes.

The dynamism of the Aryans is clear enough in their earliest and most obvious habit of invading other peoples' territories and conquering them. All of these early Aryans were intensely warlike, and their gods, myths, and heroes reflect their devotion to the martial virtues of courage, discipline, honor, the goodness of conquest, and skill in arms and sports. Virtually everywhere they moved, they conquered, though their smaller numbers in comparison with the receiving populations usually meant that sooner or later they would be absorbed into the people they overcame in battle. This was certainly their eventual fate in India and the Near East, but in Europe, despite a certain amount of racial mixture and cultural assimilation of pre-Aryan beliefs and institutions, they survived largely intact, probably because the receiving population was smaller and not as different from the conquerors as in Asia.

[270]

The dynamism of the early Aryans is also clear in their interest in travel, maritime exploration, colonization, and discovery. The Semitic Phoenicians also displayed great skill in this regard, but the Greeks equaled or excelled them in establishing colonies throughout the Mediterranean, exploring the Atlantic and African coasts, and penetrating as far as the Indian Ocean and the Far East, perhaps even circumnavigating Africa. The most famous traveler of antiquity was the historian Herodotus, who traveled all over the Near East and Egypt and invented the very concept of history in his account of his travels and the conflict between Greece and Persia.

Alexander of Macedon was a living incarnation of Aryan dynamism, conquering wherever he led his army and penetrating where no Greek had ever gone before. The racial cousins of the Greeks in late Medieval Europe and the Viking adventurers of the early middle ages surpassed the Greeks, discovering the Americas and, in the case of the Portuguese, Spanish, Dutch, French, and British, conquering new empires in Africa, Asia, and North and South America. The conquistadors of South America and the pioneers and settlers of North America reveal the same dynamic restlessness as the Germanic tribes that descended upon the Roman Empire. Their descendants today in the Aryan nations of the West stand on the edge of transcending them in their expansion into outer space itself.

[271]

But Aryan dynamism is not confined to military conquest and geographical exploration. It is also clear in the Faustian demand to understand nature. Just as Aryan warrior nomads overturned whatever cities and peoples stood in their path, so Aryan scholars and scientists, beginning with the Ionian philosophers of early Greece, have conquered nature and its mysteries, discarding myths, religions, and superstitions when they presented obstacles to their knowledge, and systematizing their discoveries and thought according to the Cosmic Order. Alexander the Great's solution of the Gordian Knot by simply slashing it to pieces with his sword is no less a racial trait of Aryans than the scientific achievements of Plato and Aristotle, Galileo and Newton, and hundreds of other scientists who were heirs of the ancient Aryans and who slashed through obscurantism and mythologies with their minds. Their descendants have cured diseases, shrunk distances, raised cities out of jungles and deserts, constructed technologies that replace and transcend human strength, restored lost languages, recovered forgotten histories, stared into the hearts of distant galaxies, and reached into the recesses of the atom. No other people has ever even dreamed of these achievements, and insofar as other peoples even know such things are possible, it is because they have learned about them from European man.

Afrocentrists, in their resentful and pathetic bitterness against whites, today pretend that it was their ancestors who created European civilization. The irony of their pretense is that their claims inadvertently acknowledge the superiority of the very civilization they hate, even as they try to claim it as their own. As for other civilized peoples, the Faustian dynamism of the Aryan race and civilization stand in stark contrast to the static primitivism and never-changing dullness that characterize the "fellahin" peoples of Asia, immersed in the fatalism and world-denying religions of the East. In travelogues and *National Geographic*, we are treated to picturesque accounts of the almost animal existences of these peoples, whose lives, work, and minds are often described as being "just what their ancestors were a thousand years ago." No phrase more accurately describes the differences between the perpetual passivity of the non-Aryan and the world-conquering activism and dynamism of the Aryans.

Critics of the Indo-Europeans often like to deflate Aryan contributions by pointing to the lateness of Aryan achievements

[272]

in ancient times and by emphasizing that most of the basic inventions that made civilization possible were of non-Aryan origin. It is true that at the time the Aryans invaded Europe, the Near East, and India, literate, urban civilizations had flourished in those regions for some centuries or millennia and that the Aryans often merely destroyed whatever lay in their paths. It is also true that inventions such as the wheel, the alphabet, the compass, the stirrup, gunpowder, and printing were not of Aryan origin.

But the point is that while other, non-Aryan civilizations may have invented these tools, only when they fell into the hands of the dynamic Aryans did they lead to enduring achievements. The Phoenicians invented the alphabet, but neither the Phoenician language nor its literature survives today. Egyptians and Sumerians built cities, empires, and great temples long before history knows of the Aryans, but today their cities, empires, and temples lie in ruins; their languages are known only to scholars, and only Indo-European scholars care about them. The Chinese may have invented the compass, gunpowder, printing, and the stirrup, but only Indo-Europeans have applied these inventions to the economic, political, and cultural conquest of the Earth. These achievements are due to the intrinsic dynamism, the Faustian creativeness, of the Indo-European mind and remain unparalleled by any other human race.

[273]

As for the lateness of Indo-European achievements, this is mainly a function of the geography of the "Aryan Homeland" in the Russian steppes, a region that furnishes few materials for building cities and lasting structures. What is striking about the Aryans, however, is that they did not remain in those regions; they conquered other, more desirable territories, took what they liked or needed from those they conquered, and over a period of about a millennium and a half after 1500 B.C. created a distinctively Aryan civilization that endures today. Those who repeat or swallow the cliché that "while white men were still running around in animal skins in northern Europe, non-Europeans were building cities and empires in Egypt and Asia" need to reflect that there were very few people at all in northern Europe at that time and that as soon as those who lived there or on the steppes became conscious of themselves as a people, they moved out of the north, conquered more comfortable climates, [274] founded what we know today as Greece, Rome, Persia, and the Indo-Aryan civilization, and proved to be unstoppable by other, more civilized peoples who are now forgotten or remembered only because Indo-European scholarship has resurrected and preserved them.

SELF-RULE

It is also the dynamism of Indo-European man that accounts for the comparative absence of "Oriental despotism" in the political history of the Aryan peoples. Both Greece and Rome were originally ruled by kings, but the kings were never absolute monarchs and were elected or confirmed by the aristocratic warrior classes. Very early in their histories, the kings were dethroned, and republics, also originally aristocratic, were established. The Roman historian Tacitus noted similar institutions among the warrior bands of the ancient Germans, whom he held up in part as models of virtue against whom the decadent Romans of his day fell short. The passive proclivities and static tendencies of non-Aryans render them easy to subjugate in such highly autocratic empires as those of Asia and ancient Egypt, imposed by slave armies often driven by whips and ruled by "god-kings" and colleges of priests armed with secret magical knowledge. It is almost impossible to dominate Aryans in this way for very long.

Greece not only gives us the word "democracy," but also the term "tyranny," which describes illegitimate rule. There is little in non-Indo-European thought similar to this concept. While Asiatic history is full of palace coups, harem intrigues, [275] assassinations, and uprisings led by one minor potentate or another against a despot, all that ever happens, from the days of the Pharaoh Akhnaton to the assassination of Anwar Sadat, is the replacement of one autocrat by another. By contrast, the histories of Greece, Rome, and Medieval and modern Europe are filled with acts of tyrannicide, political reforms, establishments of law codes and constitutions, baronial rebellions, peasants' uprisings, and eventually full-scale revolutions in which a dynamic race seeks to resist being reduced to slavery. Those despots who have gained power over Aryan peoples usually never last very long, and those who overthrow or assassinate them usually become heroic figures. The individuality and dynamism of Indo-European man simply does not tolerate one man or institution monopolizing all the power and dictating to everyone else.

This is clear enough in the histories of Greece and Rome, but it is also true of the ancient Germans. Historian Francis Owen thus describes the ancient Germanic political institutions:

> *The state, if one may use that term, was composed of all the free men of the community. On certain occasions all the free men were called together, to give assent to certain projects which had already been considered by the council of elders and leaders. The assembly had the power to reject such proposals, and instances are known when such assemblies forced on the leaders a policy of war, because peace had become monotonous, and the hope of booty was a strong lure.*
>
> *These assemblies also had the power to elect the leaders in time of war, who for the time being had almost dictatorial power.*[9]

Already in prehistoric times, then, the Germanic peoples exhibited an archaic form of republicanism that was fundamentally aristocratic in nature. The "free men" of the community did not include all inhabitants but "the great mass of independent landowners and the wealthier or more aristocratic class of recognized families, which might be called the nobility."[10] The unfree, or "thralls," had no vote or standing in the assembly. The free men were also those who bore arms, and Tacitus describes their assemblies and how they conducted them:

---

[9]   Francis Owen, *The Germanic People: Their Origin, Expansion and Culture* (New York: Dorset Press, 1990), 154.

[10] *Ibid.*, 153.

On matters of minor importance only the chiefs
debate; on major affairs, the whole community.
But even where the commons have the decision, the
subject is considered in advance by the chiefs. . . . It
is a drawback of their independent spirit that they
do not take a summons as a command; instead of
coming to a meeting all together, they waste two
or three days by their impunctuality. When the
assembled crowd thinks fit, they take their seats
fully armed. . . . If a proposal displeases them, the
people shout their dissent; if they approve, they
clash their spears. To express approbation with
their weapons is their most complimentary way of
showing agreement.[11]

When the Framers of the American Constitution [277]
guaranteed the right to keep and bear arms, "being necessary
to the security of a free State," they were following this ancient
Aryan custom of the assembly of armed free men, and much the
same custom was observed among the early Greeks and Romans.

Owen points to the dynamic quality of the ancient
Germans as the ultimate reason for their disunity as well as their
liberty, which characterized the warring kingdoms of Medieval
as well as modern Europe:

But there were other more fundamental reasons
why it was not possible to create a unified German
state. These reasons are intimately connected with
the inherent Germanic love of independence,
the spirit of individualism and the respect for

---

[11]   Tacitus, *Germany*, trans. H. Mattingly and S.A. Handford, Ch. 11.

personality. These are all highly desirable qualities,
but in an exaggerated form they do not facilitate
the formation of political unity beyond a limited
geographical area.[12]

The natural form of government among the Aryan peoples, then, appears to be this kind of aristocratic republic, tending toward democracy but with well-recognized rights and duties for non-aristocrats. A limited democracy thus has deep racial and cultural roots among Europeans, but it properly derives from those roots, not from the rootless ideologies that today have grotesquely expanded it far beyond its natural role. The natural Aryan aristocratic republicanism is a form of government encouraged by the tripartite structure of Indo-European society; by its distinctions and balances between the warrior, priestly, and producer classes; by its tendency to separate the sacred from the secular; and by the apparently innate dynamism of the Aryan race itself, which resists and rebels against any effort to impose autocratic rule or to induce the passivity that allows despotism to flourish.

[278]

It is important to note that the despotism that eventually arose in ancient Rome was based on a non-Western, Asiatic, or Egyptian model and that the ancient Greeks always feared and distrusted citizens who became "Medized" (i.e., adopted the customs of the Medes or Persians and other Asians) as people who were alienated from their own institutions and who might harbor ambitions of enslaving their own people. In Rome the great model for despotism was Egypt, after Julius Caesar dallied

---

[12]   Owen, *The Germanic People*, 155.

with Cleopatra, and both Caligula and Nero tried to imitate Egyptian and Asiatic despotism (both were assassinated). Yet the Asiatic-Egyptian model of autocracy eventually triumphed, as Rome's racial composition altered with the importation and emancipation of large masses of foreign slaves and immigrants, and it was from this model that the Roman Catholic Church developed its own ideas of papal absolutism, which in turn were copied by the monarchs of the Medieval and early modern periods. Despotism, even in its European forms, is not naturally an Indo-European institution but derives ultimately from alien peoples.

INDIVIDUALITY

[279]

The third important characteristic of the Indo-Europeans is individuality. From their earliest history they show signs of greater variation, in both physical appearance and individual behavior, than most other races. Some physical anthropologists have noted that there is more variety among Europeans than among Asiatics and Negroes, with whites exhibiting more variation in skin pigmentation, hair and eye color, height, and facial features. This physical differentiation is paralleled and perhaps causally related to their behavioral differentiation as individuals, a trait that is closely related to their dynamism as a race.

Individuality or individuation in the sense I am using it is very different from "individualism," a modern ideology that may have been encouraged by racial individuation but is not the same thing. Individualism as an ideology is the belief that the individual is sovereign, that the individual man is self-sufficient, exists only for himself and his interests, and has claims against the group (society, the race, the nation, class, religion, et cetera). This ideology is in fact subversive of group loyalty and especially of racial consciousness and allegiances, and while people with a high degree of individuality may find it attractive, they need to remember that they, like every other human being, exist because of and within a group—the family and the community, as well as larger groups such as nation, cult, class, and race.

Early Aryans, despite their tendency to individuate, were highly conscious of themselves as a distinct group. Both the Greeks and the Romans looked upon everyone else as "barbarians," and we have already seen the high degree of racial consciousness that pertained among the Indo-Aryans. Aryans were also closely attached to family units, not only the nuclear family but also the clans in which their society was organized, and clan warfare in Ireland and Scotland, family-based political factionalism among the Romans, and conflicts among the many independent city-states of ancient Greece were notorious as forces that tended to keep these populations divided. It was groups such as race, nationality, clan, community, class, and family that established the social fabric of early Aryan life, and individualism in the modern sense of a John Stuart Mill or Ayn Rand—as a belief that justifies the individual's neglecting or betraying his social bonds—did not exist.

Nevertheless, the Aryans exhibited a high degree of individuation, and this is reflected in their mythology as well as in their art. The gods and heroes of the Greeks and the Norsemen have far more distinctive personalities than such Egyptian deities as Isis and Osiris, and the stories the Greeks and Norsemen told about their gods and heroes—the embittered and wrathful Achilles and the wily Odysseus, the imperious Zeus and the dashing Apollo, the angry Ares and the comic lame god Hephaestus, the jealous Hera and the lascivious Aphrodite—are far richer than the thin tales of Egypt and Babylonia. There is also a greater emotional and narrative range—adventure, humor, love, revenge, divine punishment, and even tragic failure—in the Greek myths than in the stories of the Old Testament, which mainly illustrate man's obedience or disobedience to God and His laws.

[281]

With few exceptions, this range is also reflected in the art of the early Aryans in Europe—in the highly individuated and expressive statuary of the Greeks, as compared to the colossal but blank-faced images of the Egyptian pharaohs and Middle Eastern potentates, as well as in the highly developed literary and art forms of the later Europeans. European art and literature, far more than those of other peoples, give us the character, the individually distinctive human being, full of contradictory impulses but driven by some more than by others, characters we see in Greek drama, Homeric epic, Shakespearean plays, and the modern novel. Portraiture as well as statuary, dwelling on the individual external features to reveal the internal individual character, reflect much of the same trait, unlike the art forms of other races. Moreover, only in Western cultures has the lone hero become an ideal figure—not only the adventurer like Hercules or Theseus but also the lone explorer, the lone scientist, the lone scholar, thinker, poet, writer, often battling against daunting odds, persecution, or neglect. When Europeans invent things, they usually remember and honor the individuals who did it—the inventors who made the Industrial Revolution possible and those such as Samuel Morse, Alexander Graham Bell, Thomas Edison, the Wright brothers, and Henry Ford, who created the basic technologies of modern civilization working alone in their attics and basements.

[282]   Even the modern comic-book and film and television heroes of popular culture reveal this inherent Aryan tendency to go it alone, in the Lone Ranger, Superman and Batman, the heroes created by John Wayne and Gary Cooper, as do the myths of the American West, whether fictional, in James Fenimore Cooper's Natty Bumppo, or real, in Daniel Boone, David Crockett, Wild Bill Hickock, and Wyatt Earp. The lone Aryan hero, like Walt Disney's Davy Crockett, lives by the motto "Be sure you're right, then go ahead," a counsel of individuality, and then proceeds to fight legions of dark-looking badmen (whose black hats may symbolize non-Aryan origins), Indians, accented foreigners, or other suspiciously non-Aryan types. His ancestors Siegfried and Theseus fought and conquered the Nibelungs and the Minotaur of non-Aryan Crete in the same way.

But the Aryan hero also pays a price for his heroic individuality. He stands as the perpetual outsider, whose distinctiveness usually forbids him from enjoying a normal life with wife and children or living to a ripe old age, and eventually, in the authentic myths as opposed to TV drama, he is slain, usually by treachery. The moral of Aryan individuality is that there is no escape from the laws of the Cosmic Order, even for heroes, whose heroic transcendence of the norms that bind more mediocre men does not exempt them from the iron regularities of the universe. Individuality is not for everybody, an important distinction between the Aryan ideal and that of modern universalist individualism, and only exceptional beings can excel despite the demands it imposes on them.

[283]

Aryan individuality, then, was supposed to be a supplement to, not an adversary of, the racial and social bond, and even then it was constrained by the price that those who developed it to its highest levels would have to pay. It was never supposed to be the kind of intellectual crutch for economic greed, social inadequacy, and personal alienation and resentment that modern individualism is. But the ineradicable tendency of Aryans to individualize themselves through singular personalities, achievements, thoughts, and expressions in art and literature no doubt lies at the root of modern individualism, despite the socially pathological and destructive forms the ideology has taken, and it is in part because of his innate proclivity to individuation and individual achievement and creativity that European man has given birth to his distinctive and successful civilization.

Describing the contours of ancient history, the great American Egyptologist James Henry Breasted saw the ancient world in terms of an epochal struggle between "our ancestors," the Indo-Europeans of Europe, Persia, and India, on the one hand, and the Semitic peoples of Mesopotamia, Phoenicia, Canaan, Assyria, and Carthage, on the other:

> *The history of the ancient world, as we are now to follow it, was largely made up of the struggle between this southern Semitic line, which issued from the southern grasslands, and the northern Indo-European line, which came forth from the northern grasslands to confront the older civilizations represented in the southern line. Thus . . . we see the two great races facing each other across the Mediterranean like two vast armies stretching from Western Asia westward to the Atlantic. The later wars between Rome and Carthage represent some of the operations on the Semitic left wing, while the triumph of Persia over Chaldea is a similar outcome on the Semitic right wing.*

> *The result of the long conflict was the complete triumph of our ancestors (the Indo-European line), who conquered along the center and both wings and finally, as represented by the Greeks and Romans, gained unchallenged supremacy throughout the Mediterranean world. This triumph was accompanied by a long struggle for mastery between the members of the northern line themselves. Among them the victory moved from*

the east end to the west end of the northern line, as first the Persians, then the Greeks, and finally the Romans gained control of the Mediterranean and oriental world.[13]

In this passage, Breasted captured the grand sweep of the saga of European man and his seemingly victorious, millennial conflict with his rivals. But what he does not say, and what perhaps was not apparent to him when he wrote in the early 20th century, was that the conflict is far from over. The Roman political and military victory was not the end of the story, because the very success of Roman imperialism made possible and perhaps inevitable the eventual inundation of their people and culture by those whom they had conquered. The importation of masses of alien slaves into Italy, their eventual emancipation, and the massive immigration of foreigners from the Asiatic parts of the empire meant that the Indo-European racial and cultural base of Rome would eventually die.

[285]

The Roman poet Juvenal's famous line that "the Orontes [the main river of ancient Syria] empties its garbage into the Tiber" expresses what was happening. (It is noteworthy he did not say the Rhine or the Thames empties its garbage into the Tiber.) Not only the peoples but also the religions and the political forms of the non-Aryan East crept over the Aryan imperium. Eventually, then, the non-Aryan rivals and enemies of the Aryans triumphed through a backdoor attack that is comparable to the backhandedness by which non-Aryans overcome Aryan heroes in the old myths.

---

[13] James Henry Breasted, *The Conquest of Civilization* (New York: Literary Guild of America, 1938), 200-202.

Today, despite the conquest of virtually the entire planet by Indo-Europeans by the end of the 19th century, the same fate appears to face modern European man. Only the European nations of the United States, Canada, Australia, and New Zealand, and Europe itself face hordes of non-white immigrants who threaten to engulf us and our civilization. Having conquered them through military combat and technological and economic progress, we nevertheless face racial and cultural extinction as the perversion of our strengths into weaknesses is exploited against us and our rivals seek victory through our back doors. European man can survive today only if he begins to recognize that victory through honorable combat is not enough; he must also be prepared to meet the challenges on the level of cultural combat, and the only way he can do so is through recovery of his racial heritage, the roots of who we are and where we come from as a people.

[286]

THE ARYAN LEGACY

Throughout this essay, I have emphasized the ancient, archaic, and prehistoric expressions of the Indo-European peoples for two reasons. In the first place, examining the ancient patterns of behavior and thought among Aryans helps to exclude influences on them from more modern forces that have been acquired through the historical environment or are perhaps less "natural"—forces such as Christianity, philosophical and ethical systems, capitalism, and the modern ideologies of romanticism, individualism, socialism, capitalism, and liberalism. Secondly, by looking at the patterns of thought and behavior that seem to have been common to all or most of the early Aryan peoples, we can find what whites have in common and what distinguishes them from other races. When Aryans in Medieval Ireland exhibit myths and beliefs very similar to those of ancient India, when Greek poets express ideas similar to those of Viking sea rovers, we are transcending the extraneous influences of other cultures and races, those acquired from the social and historical environment, and the physical environment, and are coming close to fundamental racial characteristics.

This survey of the ancient Aryans may seem as though it merely recounts cultural ideas and practices rather than racial characteristics, but as Jared Taylor noted, "There is increasing evidence that personality traits . . . are under genetic control," and therefore we should expect to find that the deep cultural beliefs and practices that are common to members of a particular population that is descended from the same ancestors derive from genes carried by those ancestors. This claim cannot be proved, mainly because we obviously cannot conduct genetic analyses of ancient Aryans, but given what we now know and are increasingly learning about the role of genetic forces (and therefore race) in shaping personality (and therefore culture), it seems to follow.

[287]

In the light of what we know of the early history of the Aryan peoples, then, we should be able to distinguish between those traits that are characteristic of our race and those that are not; between those that contribute or have contributed to our success as a population and as a people and those that have been destructive; and between those that continue to serve our identity and destiny, our consciousness as a people acting in history, and those that have been distorted or exploited to thwart our identity and destiny.

In his essay "The Ways of Our People," Mr. Taylor identified by my count about 15 distinct traits that he believes constitute or derive from "a common thread to the modern characteristics of European man." In the light of what we know of early Aryan man, some of the characteristics that Mr. Taylor attributes to whites are valid, some are distortions of valid traits, and some, I believe, are merely acquisitions deriving from other forces (which is not to say that they are necessarily undesirable). But what is important is that any trait that is really a characteristic of whites must have existed long before modern culture and independently of cultural, historical, or local influences on White behavior.

[288]

Thus, several of the characteristics that Mr. Taylor attributes to whites appear to have their origin in the archaic, natural impulses of the early Aryan peoples, but it is highly misleading to say that the modern and especially American manifestations of these characteristics are distinctively Aryan, Indo-European, or white. Mr. Taylor is certainly correct that whites exhibit "an abiding sense of reciprocity, a conviction that others have rights that must be respected," but the modern expression of this trait in such institutions as democracy, free speech, and the rule of law are grotesquely distorted or exaggerated versions of the original and natural impulses.

The "sense of reciprocity" as well as the rule of law are no doubt reflections of the Aryan concept of Cosmic Order, a view of the universe that holds that both nature and man behave according to universal, perpetual laws or regular patterns and in which rights and duties are in balance. But the concept of Cosmic Order did not imply an egalitarian or homogeneous social order in which everyone is equal and there are no distinctions between groups, classes, sexes, races, and nations. Indeed, early Aryan society was hierarchical, organic, and aristocratic; the natural form of Aryan government was an aristocratic republic in which distinct classes and social groups participated and expressed their views and interests freely, and a high level of political participation was necessary for such dynamic and restless populations of independent, armed free men as the early Aryans.

[289]

The mass democracies and homogenized, produce-and-consume cultures of modern times may ultimately derive from this Aryan social and political model, but they deviate from it in important ways. Free speech, for example, certainly seems to have pertained in the tribal assemblies, and it is doubtful if the early Aryans were such bluenoses as their Victorian descendants or such totalitarians as late 20th century academics. But free speech did not include the right to commit sacrilege, subversion, or obscenity and was circumscribed by custom and the high courtesy that is universal among warrior peoples.

As noted earlier, the Aryan concept of Cosmic Order accounts for the European mental habits of universalism and objectivity. While these habits help explain European successes in science, mathematics, philosophy, ethics, and the rule of law, they also, in a misapplied and degenerate form, suggest why Europeans have shown a tendency to neglect their own racial interests and why they find developing their own racial consciousness so difficult. As Jared Taylor noted in his essay, every other race tends to think in terms of its own race and group, and, "Only whites pretend that pluralism and displacement are good things and that the measures necessary to ensure group survival may be immoral." We tend to think that way because we are naturally prone to transcend subjective and particular interests and to idealize what is objective and universal. But this misapplication of a natural and healthy Aryan instinct is not in itself natural but rather the result of ethical and philosophical confusions that have arisen in modern times.

[290]

Mr. Taylor is also correct in his remarks about sportsmanship, *noblesse oblige*, respect for foes in war, and respect for women, all of which derive from Aryan ideas about the Cosmic Order and from the warlike and heroic character of the early Aryans. All these traits reflect the nature of early Aryan warcraft—the single combat of individual champions, the unwritten and commonly understood rules of conflict, and acceptance of the terms of defeat have deep roots in the ways Aryans waged war. The comparative absence of needless brutality in Western warfare, until the advent of 20th-century democracy, may be thought to derive from Christian ethics, but long before Christianity pagan conquerors such as Alexander the Great and Julius Caesar showed far less brutality in their warfare than such paladins of non-Aryan combat as Tamerlane, Genghis Khan, the Assyrians, the Huns, or even the ancient Hebrews, for whom genocide was a regular practice.

In Aryan society, women have always enjoyed more respect, more freedom, and more individuality than in non-Aryan society, and this probably derives from the structure of their society. The relative independence and freedom that characterized the structured Aryan society would have meant that women could not simply be captured and enslaved but had to be bargained for or won, if not as individuals then as the [291] daughters of other competing warriors. Disrespect for or cruelty to a woman, like discourtesy or injury to a free man, could result in endless blood feuds. Women and goddesses in Greek and Norse myths and legends have far more personality and a far more important social role than in most non-Aryan mythologies. Certainly such practices as foot-binding, clitoridectomy, and suttee, as well as polygamy and the harem, are rare or unknown among the early Aryans. (The word "harem" has entered Western languages because Westerners lack their own word for it.)

But the natural Aryan respect for women does not mean that modern feminism is consistent with ancient Aryan views of womanhood, and despite the honor that Aryans have always paid women, they never confused honor with equality or sameness.

The assumption of the Aryan honoring of women is that women are different from men and require or deserve different treatment. It is for that very reason that modern feminists, wedded to the illusion of sexual egalitarianism, despise, ridicule, and try to abolish the expressions of male chivalry, even though, like most egalitarians, they also like to have it both ways—to abolish inequality when it offers an impediment but to insist on it when it serves their interests.

Similarly, respect for animals no doubt derives from the reliance of the Aryans on hunting and war animals, especially dogs and horses. Horses play a central role in Aryan myth, and the Indo-Europeans apparently were the first to domesticate horses and develop their use in war. There are sacred horses, horse sacrifices, horse gods, and horse burials among the Indo-European peoples. Similarly, dogs and wolves play a major role in Aryan myth, from Cerberus the three-headed dog of Hades (one for each social class perhaps) to the wolves of Odin. The individuation of Aryans may lead them to personify their animals and invest them with personalities, names, and special attributes in a way that no other race usually does.

I do not see that such traits as missionary activity, the passion to improve or change the world, the elimination of hereditary class differences, competition according to individual ability, or concern for the natural environment are particularly characteristic of Aryans, however. Some of these may be desirable traits, though they have obviously gone far beyond what was really characteristic of early Aryans and what can be useful for white racial survival. Nevertheless, some of them, such as missionary activities and crusading to change or reform society, may well ultimately derive from Aryan dynamism and expansionism, while competition according to individual merit may be a modern form of single combat and a reflection of Aryan individuality. The modern demand to eliminate hereditary class distinctions may be an exaggerated but not very healthy version of this instinct.

What is important to understand, however, is that Aryans, because of their Faustian dynamism and individuality, seem to be especially prone to misapplications of their most ennobling traits, and when the modern ideologies of egalitarianism, leveling, feminism, and universalism are joined to forces such as modern capitalism and technology, the danger of losing contact with and understanding of the natural propensities of our own racial character and of misunderstanding their limits and proper functions is great.

[293]

I do not think there is any great mystery as to how this perversion of the Aryan legacy occurred. Aryans eventually constructed societies far more complex in their economies, technologies, and ideas than any other race, and the very complexity of their societies tended to confuse and derail traditional expressions of Aryan impulses. Ambitious leaders, Aryan or not, have often exploited these complexities, and the confusions that result, for their own advantage, and the disruptions of wars, revolutions, depressions, and new technologies and social organizations that periodically afflict Western society have added to the alienation of modern European man from his natural inclinations and ancient heritage.

It ought to be obvious that we cannot expect to restore the warrior cultures of the early Aryans, their archaic religions and mythologies, and their social and political customs. But we can work to correct the misapplications of our talents and traits, to eradicate the confusions and degenerations of modern mass democracy and culture, and eventually to restore or create anew a social, political, and cultural order that incorporates and reflects the healthy and natural instincts of our race. What we can do is learn from these ancient and noble warriors and their courage, their irrepressible restlessness and dynamism, and their heroically relentless realism; from them we can remember who we are and where we come from, what our most natural inclinations are and how those inclinations can help us or harm us, and, most of all, how we can make the enduring characteristics of our race serve us again in our endless quest to meet the destiny of European man. ࿐

[*web*]
www.RadixJournal.com
www.WashSummit.com

[*email*]
Hello@WashSummit.com

[*mail*]
Radix Journal
P.O. Box 100563
Arlington VA 22210

www.ingramcontent.com/pod-product-compliance
Lightning Source LLC
Chambersburg PA
CBHW050644270326
41927CB00012B/2869